*For Bread Alone*

Mohamed Choukri

*For Bread Alone*

*Translated and with an Introduction by*

Paul Bowles

Saqi Books

British Library Cataloguing-in-Publication Data
A catalogue record for this book is available from the
British Library

ISBN 0 86356 138 1

This edition first published 1993 by
Saqi Books
26 Westbourne Grove
London W2 5RH

# Introduction

Because I have translated several books from the Arabic I want to make a clear differentiation between the earlier volumes and the present work. The other books were spoken onto tape and the words were in the colloquial Arabic called Moghrebi. *For Bread Alone* is a manuscript, written in classical Arabic, a language I do not know. The author had to reduce it first to Moroccan Arabic for me. Then we used Spanish and French for ascertaining shades of meaning. Although exact, the translation is far from literal.

It has been my experience that the illiterate, not having learned to classify what goes into his memory, remembers everything. This too is a technique. Total recall is like perfect pitch: it means nothing in itself, but it can be extremely helpful to the writer who uses it professionally. It seems almost a stroke of good luck that Choukri's encounter with the written word should have come so late, for by then his habits of thought were already fully formed; the educative process did not modify them. As a writer, then, he is in an enviable position, even though he paid a high price for it in suffering.

Choukri grew up under conditions of poverty excessive even for Morocco. Eight of his brothers and sisters died of malnutrition and neglect. Another brother was killed outright by Choukri's father in an access of hunger and desperation. Mohamed and one or two others managed to survive, even under these worst possible circumstances. *For Bread Alone* records his struggle for survival, up to the time the young man made the resolve to become literate. To have taken and implemented such a decision at the age of twenty is unusual.

To have passed in the space of five years from learning the letters of the alphabet to writing poems and stories is even more unexpected.

Paul Bowles
Morocco 1973

# Glossary

*aaita:* a card game
*alpargatas:* old-fashioned Spanish canvas slippers
*baqal:* a grocer or grocery
*bodega:* a Spanish tavern
*cargador* (pl. *cargadores*): a hand-porter
*dfin:* a woman's garment of sheer material, worn over the caftan
*djellaba:* a long, hooded garment worn by men and women
*djinn* (pl. *djenoun*): a spirit able to appear in human and animal forms, and having supernatural power over human beings
*fjer:* the pre-dawn prayer at the mosque
*hammam:* a public bath
*harira:* a thick soup
*jefatura:* the central police station
*kif:* a type of hashish found in North Africa
*limonada:* bottled soda water flavoured with lemon
*mahia:* an *eau de vie*, generally made from figs or dates, distilled by the Moroccan Jews
*majoun:* a paste made of hashish
*maricón* (pl. *maricones*): an effeminate man; homosexual
*paseo:* a walk or stroll; a drive
*qahouaji:* a man who prepares and serves tea (or coffee) in an Arab café
*sala:* sitting-room
*sebsi:* a *kif* pipe
*surah* (pl. *surat*): a version of the Koran
*taifor:* a very low, round table
*tajine:* a stew

*tapas: hors d'oeuvres* served with drinks in Arab and Spanish cafés

*tas:* a washing basin brought to the table before a meal

*tolba:* Koranic students

*zib:* penis

*zigdoun:* a woman's garment, akin to a Mother Hubbard


*A Note on Pronunciation*

English-speaking readers should note that the *ch* in North African words is pronounced as *sh* in English (e.g. Choukri and Larache are pronounced Shoukri and Larashe).

# 1

Surrounded by the other boys of the neighbourhood, I stand crying. My uncle is dead. Some of them are crying, too. I know that this is not the same kind of crying as when I hurt myself or when a plaything is snatched away. Later on I began to see that many people cried. That was at the time of the great exodus from the Rif. There had been no rain, and as a result there was nothing to eat.

One afternoon I could not stop crying. I was hungry. I had sucked my fingers so much that the idea of doing it again made me sick to my stomach. My mother kept telling me: Be quiet. Tomorrow we're leaving for Tangier. There's all the bread you want there. You won't be crying for bread any more, once we get to Tangier.

My little brother Abdelqader was too sick to cry as I did. Look at your little brother, she told me. See how he is. Why can't you be like him?

I stare at his pallid face and his sunken eyes and stop crying. But after a few moments I forget to be inspired by his silence, and begin once more to cry.

When my father came in I was sobbing, and repeating the word *bread* over and over. Bread. Bread. Bread. Bread. Then he began to slap and kick me, crying: Shut up! Shut up! Shut up! If you're hungry, eat your mother's heart. I felt myself lifted into the air, and he went on kicking me until his leg was tired.

We were making our way towards Tangier on foot. All along the road there were dead donkeys and cows and horses. The dogs and crows were pulling them apart. The entrails were soaked in blood and pus, and worms crawled out of them. At night when we were tired we set up our tent. Then we listened to the jackals baying.

When someone died along the road, his family buried the body there in the place where he had died. After we had set out Abdelqader began to cough, and the cough grew worse as we went along. Fearful for his sake and my own, I said to my mother:

Will Abdelqader die too?

No, of course not. Who said he was going to die?

My uncle died.

Your brother's not going to die. He's sick, that's all.

I did not see as much bread in Tangier as my mother had promised me I should. There was hunger even in Eden, but at least it was not a hunger that killed. One day when the hunger had grown too strong, I went out to Aïn Ketiout to look in the garbage dump for bones and ends of dry bread. I found another boy there before me. He was barefoot and his clothes were in shreds. His scalp was covered with ringworm, his arms and legs scarred with sores.

The garbage in the middle of town is a lot better than it is here, he said. Nazarene garbage is the best.

After that I wandered further afield in search of food, sometimes alone, sometimes with another boy who was looking for the same thing. One day I found a dead hen. I seized it and hugged it close, for fear someone would snatch it away.

Mother in the city, Abdelqader propped against the cushions. His huge eyes, half shut, watched the entrance door. He sees the hen, and his eyes open wide. He smiles, his thin face flushes, he moves, coughs. I find the knife. I turn towards the east, as my mother always does when she is about to pray.

I said: *Bismillah. Allahou akbar.* And I kill it as I have seen grown-ups do it.

I drew the knife back and forth across its throat until its head fell off. I was waiting to see the blood come out.

I massage the bird a little. Maybe it will come out now.

A few drops of blackish blood appeared in its open gullet. In the Rif I had watched them kill a sheep. They put a bowl under its throat to catch the blood. When the bowl was full they gave it to my mother, who was sick in bed. They held her down and made her drink it. Her face and clothing were smeared with it. Why doesn't the blood come out of the hen the way it did with the sheep?

I began to pull off the feathers.

I hear her voice. What are you doing? Where did you steal that?

I found it. It was sick. But I killed it before it died.

You're crazy. She pulled it away from me. People don't eat carrion.

My brother and I exchanged a glance of regret. The hen was lost.

Each afternoon my father comes home disappointed. Not a movement, not a word, save at his command, just as nothing can happen unless it is decreed by Allah. He hits my mother. Several times I have heard him tell her: I'm getting out. You can take care of those two whelps by yourself.

He pours some snuff onto the back of his hand and sniffs it, all the while talking to himself. Bitch. Rotten whore. He abuses everyone with his words, sometimes even Allah.

My little brother cries as he squirms on the bed. He sobs and calls for bread.

I see my father walking towards the bed, a wild light in his eyes. No one can run away from the craziness in his eyes or get out of the way of his octopus hands. He twists the small head furiously. Blood pours out of the mouth. I run outdoors and hear him stopping my mother's screams with kicks in the face. I hid and waited for the end of the battle.

The voices of the night, far away and near. For the first

time I realize that I can hear better at night than by day. I looked up at the sky. Allah has turned on the lights. Clouds sail across the face of the big lamp. My mother's ghost appears. She is calling me in a low voice, searching for me in the darkness as she sobs. Why is she so weak? Why isn't she strong enough to hit him as hard as he hits her? Men hit. Women scream and weep.

Mohamed! Come here! There's nothing to be afraid of. Come here.

It gave me great pleasure to see her knowing that she could not see me. A little god.

After a while I said: Here I am.

Come here.

No. He'll kill me. He killed Abdelqader.

Don't be afraid. Come. He's not going to kill you. Come on. But be quiet, so you won't wake the neighbours.

He was in the room taking snuff and sobbing. I was astonished. He kills Abdelqader and then he cries about it.

They sat up all night, weeping silently. I went to sleep and left them sobbing together. In the morning we cried again, all of us. It was the first time I had seen a funeral. My father walked behind the old man who carried the litter, and I followed at the back, lame and barefoot.

They drop him into the wet hole. I cry and shiver. There is a mass of coagulated blood beside his mouth.

On the way back home the old man noticed the blood coming up between my toes, and spoke to me in Riffian. What's that?

He stepped on some glass, said my father. He doesn't even know how to walk. He's an idiot.

Did you love your brother very much? the old man asked me.

Yes, I said. And my mother loved him more. She loved him more than she did me.

All people love their children, he said.

I thought of how my father had twisted Abdelqader's neck. I wanted to cry out: He killed him! Yes. He killed him. I saw him kill him. He did it. He killed him! I saw him. He twisted his neck around, and the blood ran out of his mouth. I saw it. I saw him kill him! He killed him!

To ease the unbearable hatred I felt for my father I began to cry. Then I was afraid he was going to kill me too. He began to scold me in a low voice loaded with menace. Stop that. You cried enough at home.

Yes, said the old man. Stop crying. Your brother is with Allah. With the angels.

I hate even the old man who buried my brother.

Every day he bought tobacco and a sack of white bread. He goes somewhere far from Tangier to barter with the Spanish soldiers in their barracks. Each afternoon he comes in carrying uniforms. He sells them in the Zoco de Fuera to workmen and poor people.

One afternoon he did not come back. I went to bed, leaving my mother bathed in tears. We waited three days. I wept with her, certain that I did it only to console her. I did not ask her why she was crying. She does not love him, I know.

I find out why she is crying only when she tells me. Here we are, all alone. Who's going to help us? We don't know anybody in this city. Your grandmother Rouqaiya, your Aunt Fatima and your Uncle Driss have all gone to Oran. Your father deserted from the Spanish army. They were looking for him. They must have found him.

We learned later that this had been the case. He had refused to sell a blanket to a Moroccan soldier who wanted it at a very low price, and the soldier had denounced him to the authorities.

She goes to the city in search of work. She comes back disappointed, just as my father used to do when we first arrived in Tangier. She sits biting her nails distractedly. She sobs. Sorcerers make her talismans to wear around her neck; perhaps my father will get out of prison and she will find work. She says her prayers and lights candles at the tombs of the saints. She looks for luck at the fortune-teller's. There is no way out of prison, there is no work, no luck, save by order of Allah and Mohamed his prophet; this is what she says. I began to think: Why doesn't Allah give us our good luck the way he gives it to other people?

I passed the question to my mother. That's something we can't ask, she said. He knows much better than we do, and when he wants us to know, he'll tell us.

She sold some things we did not need, and sent me with some other boys of the neighbourhood to pick some rosemary for her. I was afraid the boys were going to hurt me. There was no friend among them who would come to my aid if they should all jump on me at once. It had often happened. I would get into a fight with one, and they would all attack me. They helped each other.

I stayed well behind them in the middle of the road. Then I turned and went down to the city. I like the way it moves. In the Zoco de Fuera I filled my stomach with cabbage leaves and orange peel.

A policeman is chasing another boy, older than I. Not much distance between them. I imagine I am the boy. I felt myself panting with him. People were crying: He's going to catch him! He's going to catch him! He's going to catch him! There he goes! He's got him!

I trembled. I felt fear, as if I had been caught myself. I would have asked Allah not to let them catch him. But they have already caught him. I hate the people who wanted the policeman to catch him.

A breathless European woman arrived and stood behind the small group of people that had been watching the capture.

It was one like that, she said.

All he left was the handle of the bag, someone was saying.

A second later I felt the blow of a nightstick on my buttocks. I leapt into the air, crying out in Riffian: *Ay mainou! Ay mainou!*

I imagined myself cursing the man. There were two other policemen now, beating the boys and pushing the men. Some of the more poorly dressed men got blows, too. I had thought that the police beat you and took you to jail only if you had killed or robbed somebody, or drawn his blood in a fight.

I went to the graveyard in Bou Araqia. Large bunches of myrtle had been left on some of the richer tombs. I gathered them up and carried them to my brother's grave. There were many graves without tiles marking them, and without myrtle on them, like my brother's. A mound of earth and two stones of different shapes, one for the head and one for the feet. The sight of the neglected graves hurt me. I thought: Even here in the cemetery there are rich people and poor people.

I found big clumps of rosemary growing there among the graves. There were three men passing a bottle from one to the other and drinking a dark liquid from it. One of them called to me: Hey! Come here, boy! *Agi!*

I was afraid. I fled.

At lunch she said to me: That rosemary is very sweet.

We both had good appetites.

Yes, it's sweet, I said.

Where did you pick it?

In the graveyard at Bou Araqia.

The graveyard!

Yes.

She stares at me open-mouthed.

I went to see Abdelqader's grave. I put a little myrtle on it. The mound is not very high now. If it stays the way it is, all the dirt is going to be gone, and we won't be able to tell it apart from the others.

She stopped eating and her features froze.

I went on: There's lots of that rosemary there growing around the old graves.

Don't you know you're not supposed to eat anything that grows in a cemetery?

Why not?

She looked at me anxiously. I go on eating with relish. She is worried. Her appetite is gone. I thought for a moment that she was going to vomit. She seized the plate from which I was eating and took it away, saying in Riffian: Eat yourself up.

After a moment she asked me: Where did you get the myrtle?

Off some other graves. They had lots of it.

She stared. Tomorrow you're going back to the cemetery and take the myrtle to the same graves where you found it. Don't you know what graves are? And be careful nobody sees you putting the myrtle back. We'll buy our own myrtle for your brother. We'll make him a beautiful grave when we've saved a little money.

It was a great relief not to have my father in the house, but the small amount of money he had left there was soon gone. I longed to grow up quickly so I would be able to do the same sort of work he had done. In my fantasies it was taken for granted that he would never return. It was inadmissible that he should ever again have a part in the life I shared with my mother.

Sometimes she takes me with her to the Zoco de Fuera. We buy a huge pile of dry bread from the beggars. We take it home to boil in water, sometimes with a little oil and pepper, sometimes without. Early one morning she said to me: I'm going to the market to buy and sell vegetables. You stay here. Take good care of the house. Don't go and play with the other boys and leave the door open for thieves to come in.

I began to be aware of certain differences between myself and the other boys of the neighbourhood, even though some of them were poorer than I. I had seen one of them pull chicken bones out of a garbage pail and suck them. The garbage here is good, he had said.

I hear them talking among themselves about me.

He's a Riffian.

They're starving to death. They're all criminals.

He can't even speak Arabic.

The Riffians are all sick this year.

The cows and sheep they brought with them are sick too.

We don't eat them. They're the ones who eat them. Rotten people eat rotten meat.

If one of their cows or sheep or goats dies, they eat it instead of throwing it out. They eat everything.

The Djibli boy, as well as the Riffian boy, is an object of this kind of scorn, but the scorn is not expressed in the same way or with the same gestures. In general the Djibli is considered an oaf. 'The treacherous Riffian and the gullible Djibli.' I had heard people say it.

Next to our house there is a small orchard. The big pear tree attracts me to it every day. Early one morning the owner of the orchard caught me poking a long pole into the tree and shaking the biggest and ripest pears from the branches. He drags me along the ground and I struggle to get free. At the moment I gave up hope, I felt the urine begin to run out of me into my wide Arab trousers. I was crying, even though he was not hitting me.

His wife had a bright smile.

This is the flea that's been ruining our pear tree! he cried. He's like a rat. He spoils more than he eats.

Where's your mother, my son? The woman's voice was sweet, and it soothed my fear.

She went to sell vegetables in the market, I sobbed.

Stop crying. And your father?

He's in jail.

In jail! Poor man. Why did they put him in jail?

The question bothered me. She repeated it, caressing my cheek. Tell me. Why is your father in jail?

I felt that a truthful reply would reflect upon the family name. I don't know why, I said. My mother knows.

A conversation followed between the man and his wife. Then their daughter appeared, barefoot, her head enveloped in a cloth, and her long fingers dripping with water. They were discussing the possibility of locking me up until my mother got back. I can see that the two women feel sorry for me. But the man, half in jest, half in earnest, wants me punished. He made me go into a dark room piled with old furniture. And don't cry, you hear? he said as he shut the door. Or I'll take this cane to you.

17

It was the first time I had been shut into a room. I realized that not only those of my own family, but other people as well, had power over me. And then I understood that the big sweet pears belonged to the people who had imprisoned me. Why did we come all the way from the Rif when others stayed behind in their own country? Why does my father go to prison, and my mother go to sell vegetables, leaving me alone and with nothing to eat, when this man stays at home with his wife? Why can't we have what other people have?

Through a hole in the door I watched the girl as she gave the floor a vigorous scrubbing. She was still barefoot; her flimsy skirts were pulled up, revealing her thighs. As she bends over, I see her small breasts shaking back and forth. They appear and disappear inside the low-necked garment. As they tipped forward, the breasts moved like two bunches of grapes. The white cloth around her head, stained with henna, was like the outer leaves of a cabbage. I rapped on the door, softly, for I was afraid. I watched her, timing my heart to her movements. She turned towards the door, still bent over, still scrubbing. I imagined myself calling to her: Come and open this door! And I continued to call silently. Decide to come.

She dropped the rag on the floor and stood up, shaking her hands. She put her hands on her hips and bent backwards, and a faint grimace of pain flickered over her face. Here she is, coming towards the door. My heart beat faster and I began to tremble. She opened the door. What do you want? Her voice was friendly.

If my mother comes home and doesn't find me there, she's going to hit me, I began.

She pulled her clothing down to cover her fleshy legs. For a moment she gazed at me with compassion. I looked back at her humbly. She buttoned up the neck of her garment and stood erect. I see the two dark grapelike points of her breasts through the gauzy white cloth.

Are you going to knock the pears off our tree again with your pole?

No. You can kill me yourself if you find me doing it again.

She smiled. I did not dare to smile. She forgave me. Quickly I ran out. Behind me I heard her voice: Come here! Are you hungry?

I hesitated, torn between two desires. Then I said: No.

She understood the cause of my trembling, and insisted that I wait a moment. Her parents were not in the house. I looked at the pear tree, loving it and hating it. I was thinking that from then on I was not going to have any more of those sweet pears.

She handed me a piece of bread that dripped with honey. Here. If you're hungry come back to our house. Haven't you got any shoes?

No. My mother told me she was going to buy me some.

She continued to look at me, smiling at me from where she stood. Before I had run out of sight I saw her wave to me. I smiled and waved back.

Men are harder than women, I thought. I wished that the girl were my sister, and that the house and the orchard were ours. It also occurred to me that the man was not as bad as my father.

He follows us wherever we go. He whispers words into her ear, but I cannot hear what they are. She walks ahead, leaving him behind. We cross to the opposite pavement, she holding my hand. Sometimes she pulls me along roughly. I see him, still following us doggedly. He is laughing. She is angry. I am unhappy.

What does that man want? I asked her.

Shut up!

I look back at him and see him smiling. He goes on following us. What does this man want of my mother? Does he want to kidnap her? A kidnapper! No, he's probably a thief. He looks bad.

I held her hand tightly. Why are you squeezing my hand so hard? she demanded. I'm not going to run away from you.

Go away! I shouted at him, furious. *Allah inaalik!*

He's smiling. He smiles at my mother and me, and I stare

angrily into his face. I told you to shut up, she said.

In my head I grew angry with her too. I try to take care of her and she tells me to shut up.

She stopped to chat with a woman she knew. I saw the man going along, farther and farther away from us. The woman patted my head and ran her rough hand over my face. I let go of my mother's hand so she would be free to talk, and wrapped my arms around her legs.

Why is your Mohamed so unhappy? the woman asked my mother.

My mother looked down at me and cupped the back of my neck in her hand. The gesture made me feel better.

He's always like this. He's a strange boy.

They said goodbye to one another. Kiss Lalla el Ouiza's hand, my mother told me.

Obediently I kissed the hard hand she held out.

I noticed that my mother's belly had begun to swell. Some days she does not go to the market. She stays at home, and she vomits now and then. She is pale and her legs are swollen. She sobs. Her belly swells and swells. I began to wonder if it would burst. I no longer noticed her sobs. Each day I am growing harder and gloomier. Hard, hard. Sad. I have forgotten how to play.

One night, half asleep, I was carried to another house, where I fell asleep again in the midst of three other children. In the morning, the neighbour woman, whose husband had been killed in an accident at work a few days earlier, came to me and said: Your mother has a baby girl. Now you have a sister.

Once a week my mother goes to see my father in the jail. Sometimes she comes back weeping. I began to understand that women cry more than men. They start and stop easily, like children. Sometimes they are upset when you think they are going to be pleased. And they laugh when you think they are going to be angry. And often it's hard to tell whether they are sad or happy. When are they going to laugh and when are they going to cry?

I stay at home to take care of my sister Khemou. I know how to amuse her, but not how to make her stop crying. It bothers me finally, and I go outside. I leave her there crying, paddling her crooked arms and legs, like a tortoise on its back. When I go in the next time I find her asleep, or merely smiling. Usually asleep, while the flies buzz around her face, already irritated by mosquito bites. At night the mosquitoes and in the daytime the flies.

My sister grows. Now my mother does not cry so much. She has fewer complaints. I am becoming meaner, sometimes with my mother and sometimes with the boys in the street. When I feel myself overcome, either by her or by them, I break things, or throw myself down screaming insults and hitting myself.

She began to take me and Khemou to market with her. Khemou drinks at my mother's breast. I usually look for my food far from either of them. Sometimes I beg and sometimes I steal.

For the first time I dared say to her: If you don't let me do what I want, some day I'll go away from this house, and never come back.

Aha, the beetle talking! If you're like that already, what will you be like later?

One morning as we walked through the Zoco de Fuera, my father bore down on us. He was on his way to find us, and he was with a woman who was going to show him where we lived now. My mother began to cry, there in the market. Why is she crying about him? I wondered. He's like a wild animal, and he's always in a bad temper.

That night I fell asleep as they argued and wrangled. In the morning my mother did not go to the market. Instead she went to the *hammam*. Later I found her making up her face. She looked very happy. Then when my father went out I saw her crying again. I did not know any woman could cry so much. I decided to ask her what was the matter. She told me that my father had gone out to look for the soldier who had denounced him, and now they were going to kill each other.

I hoped he would find the soldier so that we could go on living in the house without him. One of them would kill the other, and that was all I wanted. I like it when he's absent, and hate it when he's in the house.

In the afternoon he came back dejected, giving off a smell of wine. I heard my mother say: You've been drinking, haven't you?

He mumbled a few words and sat down exhausted. He is sad because he has not found his enemy, and I am sad because he has come back.

I heard them talking about a trip to Tetuan. They were still discussing it when I went to sleep. I woke in the night with a full bladder. The sound of kisses, like the clapping of hands. Hard breathing, tender murmurs. They like each other. I hate their love. Flesh clapping. Pfou! She tells lies. I'll never believe her again.

No. Not like that.

What are they doing?

Like this.

No! No! It hurts. Like this. Like this. That's better. No, no! Like this. Yes, that's right.

Breathing, kisses, groans, breathing, kisses, groans. They are biting each other. They are devouring one another, licking each other's blood.

Mmmmm!

He's stabbed her.

A long soft moan.

He's killed her.

I feel my bladder emptying itself. The warm liquid running between my thighs feels good.

The day before we left for Tetuan I saw the girl who had given me the bread and honey. I told her about the trip we were going to make. She took me home to her house with her. There I ate brown bread with butter and honey. And she gave me a large apple, and filled my pockets with almonds. She washed my face and hands. Then she combed my hair for me and cut it, rubbing her fingers over my cheek as she did so, and put eau de cologne on me. She brought out a small mirror and told me to look into it. I obeyed, but I looked more intently at her than at myself.

She took my head between her hands, the way I would have taken a small bird so as not to injure it. First she rubs my cheek tenderly and then she tickles it with her fingertips. When she said goodbye she kissed me on the cheek and then on the lips. She was a sister to whom my mother had not given birth.

The day we left for Tetuan, I remembered Abdelqader's grave. No one would put water on it, or sprigs of myrtle, and there were still no tiles around it. His grave will be invisible among all the others. It will get lost, the way little things always disappear among the big ones.

# 2

We had found a house by an orchard in the quarter of Aïn Khabbès. My mother went back to selling vegetables in the street. This suited my father, who liked nothing better than to sit in the garden of the Feddane, deep in conversation with the wounded veterans of the Spanish Civil War. I ran errands for our Spanish neighbours. My sister rolled on the floor and tried to learn to walk. Soon my father found me work in a nearby café. My day lasted from six in the morning until after midnight. Each month my father went and collected the thirty pesetas I had earned with my work. He did not give me any of it. He was using me, and I hated him for it, as I hated everyone who used others in this way. My father uses my mother and me. The man who runs the café uses me, too, since he makes me work longer than I should. But what can I do?

I can steal. I can steal from anybody who uses me.

I began to think of stealing as a way of regaining that which had been taken from me. The café had two separate clienteles, the daytime one and the night-time one, but on holidays they mingled. Then those of the daytime learned what went on at night, and those of the night-time asked for news of the daytime. I smoked in secret. The first time I ate a piece of *majoun* I fainted. Later I vomited what looked like moss. I went on being sick for several days, and life looked strangely different during that time. Illness makes one more alone. I understood that I was only I, face to face with myself.

The men in the café encouraged me to smoke *kif* and eat *majoun*. Daytimes it was *kif* and work, but at night it was *majoun* and fun. One of them said: It's only the first time you take it that you throw up. He was right. I never felt sick again. Then when I drank wine for the first time, and was immediately ill, they told me the same thing about wine. The smokers and drinkers are always right. I had no trouble the second time I tried wine. The café owner saw nothing strange about a twelve-year-old boy who got drunk and smoked *kif*. He too drank and took hashish. I knew that what interested him was making money.

Some nights I slept on a bench in the café. Other times it was at the Spanish bakery nearby. One night I watched the workers amuse themselves. Five or six of them took hold of Yazidi the baker and got him to the floor. They gagged him with a handkerchief so he could not bite them. Then one of them let down his trousers and, squatting over Yazidi, began to rub his buttocks, his scrotum and his sex against Yazidi's nose. Since I was afraid they might do the same thing to me, I decided to get out of the bakery quickly. The dangers of the streets on the way home were preferable, even though the distance seemed great at night when it was dark, and I was frightened.

The café owner lived in a house that was built against the café. Sometimes he would start to get drunk there, and go on to finish his spree at a brothel in Tetuan where he would stay until the next day, or even two or three days if he went to a brothel in another town. During this time his absence made it possible for me to indulge my taste for thievery.

I got into the habit of going into his house whenever I felt like it, and eating at table with his sons. When I was drunk, I slept at the café, otherwise I slept in the same room with them. I saw that the man beat his wife and children the same way as my father did. Even so, he was less bestial. Several times I saw him kiss his sons, and he held long, calm conversations with his wife. My father could speak only in shouts and slaps. Sometimes I did not go home to see my parents for more than a week. This way I escaped from the discord and wrangling.

I grew very thin and sickly. I saw that my mother's belly was swelling again, and I thought to myself: This time I'm not going to stay at home to take care of the baby that's going to come out. The belly grows, the time of screaming comes nearer. One day there it will be. Ouaaaaah! I stopped working. During the days while I was getting well, I spent my time catching birds in the orchard. I made a swing out of a heavy rope and hung it from a tree. Surprise! The swing gives me a delicious sensation. My sex stands up all by itself when I climb onto the swing. In the orchard there was a big tank full of water, and there I learned to swim. Early in the morning I would go out and look for things to steal: fruit, eggs, or hens. Whatever I found I sold to the *baqal* in our quarter. Each day the sight of certain living creatures produced great excitement in me: hens, goats, dogs and calves. Many hens died as a result of my experiments. I would have to muzzle a dog, or tie up a calf, but there was no need to take such precautions with a goat or a hen, and these were more satisfactory. I began to have pains in my chest, and mentioned them. They told me: You're growing up, that's all. I have a disturbing sensation in my nipples and in my sex, and when I squeeze the milk out of my sex, I feel as if I were being torn to pieces inside my body.

One morning I climbed a fig tree, and through its branches I saw Asiya, the daughter of the man who owned the orchard. She was coming along slowly towards the tank. Bad luck, I thought. She's going to see me up here, and tell that father of hers. He's like my father; he never smiles. She looked this way and that, stopped walking, and listened to the sounds around her. Then she continued hesitantly, looking in every direction as she went, taking her steps with great care. She untied the sash of her pyjamas and pulled off the jacket like a bird getting

27

ready to fly. The whiteness of her skin burst forth. Again she turns and looks around. She is not in a hurry. She seems to be listening for something. I am overcome by anxiety. One fig falls out of my hand, and the one in my mouth suddenly goes down my throat. The basket leans to one side, and half the figs fall out. The sun has already appeared. The circle of red on the shining white mist of the sky was like an egg that had been broken onto a blue plate. The animals and birds and insects have begun their morning praise of Allah. When a donkey brays, its sound drowns out the songbirds, doves and roosters. She is undressing. Asiya, she is taking everything off. Her pyjamas slide down like a curtain falling. She's all undressed. Asiya, she's naked. Asiya's naked. How bright she is! Full breasts, their points protruding. Below, black hairs outline a triangle. My trousers are too tight. They hurt in front. She takes two slow steps towards the tank. My discomfort in front grows worse and worse. Her long hair covers her from behind. She stoops over, and I am afraid she may break in two. Now her hair falls forward over her shoulders and no longer hides her back. Below the point where her white flesh divides there is a slight darkness. My mouth tastes as though I had been eating honey, and every part of me itches. My nipples ache and my trousers hurt. A sweet seizure, a feeling of release, and then delicious relaxation. I'm going to fall out of the tree. I almost fell. She still hesitates, then she steps into the water. The stone steps are slippery. I am afraid she may fall. I worry. She looks at the water and all around at the orchard. She scoops up water to her armpits and lets it run down. She lets it run over her breasts, and splashes a little between her thighs. Then she pours it over her head and jumps in.

I climb down from the tree and creep along the ground until I reach the pyjamas, which I seize and quickly hide among the bushes. Then I crawl again to the tree and climb back up, waiting and grinning. I devour the figs greedily, delighted with my game. She swims beautifully. The way she plunges beneath the surface and bobs up again reminds me of a wild duck. I had heard about the swimming prowess of mermaids, and it seemed to me that she was like one of them. She is on her belly, her back, now on one side, now the other. She pushes to the bottom of the pool, and comes up dancing like an empty bottle on top of the water. What a delight it is that she should not know I am here, that she should imagine herself completely alone!

She climbs out shivering, stares in astonishment, and begins to search wildly for her pyjamas, darting this way and that distractedly. When she sights them, she puts them on and dashes through the orchard. I am left laughing in the tree, but once again a donkey covers all sounds with his braying.

In the night I dreamed of Asiya, still unfastening her belt, still floating naked and darting like an eel along the bottom of the tank. I was swimming along with her, above her, below her and on both sides of her. We stood upright in the water for a moment, kissed and sank.

A little girl named Mounat pulled up her dress, crouched, and made water. She did not know I was watching. I wondered why her pink thing had no hairs around it. It was not pretty when she squatted down: it was as ugly as a toothless old mouth. And I saw our neighbour Saida changing her clothes. Her belly sticks out, not something you would want to touch. Her breasts are flabby. So much hanging flesh disgusts me. Things became clearer. I begin to make comparisons between beautiful things and ugly ones. It seemed to me that unless women had bodies like Asiya's, they were ugly.

I am bothered every day by my sex. I scratch it slowly with my fingers as if it were a pimple not yet ready to burst. Then it fills and grows hard, until it is sweating and panting. Unless I reach pleasure during my reverie, I feel pain like two stones. I conjure up the picture of Asiya's body. Never have I seen anything so lovely and desirable. I kiss her, suck her breasts, and she caresses me with her hands and her lips. I imagine her, I keep imagining her, I maintain her picture in the dream by an effort of will, until the liquid is forced out and I disappear into delight.

When I told Asiya that it was I who had hidden her pyjamas, she chased me. I can jump over things that she has to go around. I turned to look. She had almost caught up with me. I stumbled and fell, and she fell on top of me. I tried to get up, but she had hold of me. Again we rolled on the ground. Then she stopped the game, looking suddenly ashamed. I thought: I too am going to be stronger than a woman.

I use up a great many boxes of matches pursuing my newest pastime. I sit on the edge of the tank and wait for the eels to come out of the crevices at the bottom of the tank. I twist five or six wax matches together, light them, and throw them at the moving eels. Still tossing matches, I follow their frantic course until they wriggle back into their holes. The sight of the small flames falling in the air together with the undulating movements of the eels, these things calm my resentment and anxiety.

I sat there now as usual, tossing bunches of matches into the water. One bunch fell out of my hand before I was able to throw it. I made another bunch and lighted it, without looking to see what had become of the first, which had landed on the ground. Next I heard the sound of canes crackling. I tried to put the fire out by throwing rocks at it, but it only blazed higher. Then I ran and hid in the stable. I heard voices crying for water, and burrowed deeper into the hay, pondering my bad luck. When night came, I crept into the stall where the cows slept. I made one of them stand up, and I patted her head and smoothed her hide. Then I rubbed her udder, and she let me suck on it. After three days of fear and watchfulness in the lanes and alleys of the quarter, and three nights of milk-sucking in the security of the stable, I fell into the trap my father had set for me. The neighbours had to break the bolt on our front door in order to deliver me and my mother from the blows of his military belt. My body was covered with bleeding welts, and one of her eyes was swollen shut. It was many nights before I could find a comfortable position to sleep in. I longed to be able to sleep in the air. My wounds hurt, my bones ache, and I can feel the fever burning in my head.

I went back to get drunk and smoke *kif* in the café. There I saw Fatima, the café owner's daughter, bending over as she did the washing, with her clothing hitched up under her sash in front. She seemed older now, and bigger and stronger than I, and I looked at her with longing. My father's rough treatment of me always served only to increase the rage of my desire. The girl turned towards me with a smile. I looked at her, and in my mind's eye I see a gust of wind arrive, and lift her filmy garments. Asiya is prettier than she is. But Fatima is in front of me. She stood up straight and stretched. Then she put her arm behind her back, wincing a bit. I was staring wistfully at her full bare thighs. Quickly she let her skirts fall to cover her knees.

I imagined myself going over to her and slapping her in the face. Then I would pull the skirt up again, and she would yank it down angrily. I would hit her again and lift it up. She would scream with rage, and I would set her clothes on fire. The flames as they burned her underwear delighted me.

Suddenly she demanded: What is it?

Disappointed, I said: There's no more sugar in the café.

She looked at me piercingly. Don't you know where we keep the sugar?

I glared at her.

What's the matter with you today? she said, staring at me. I did not reply, and she added: You're strange today.

I went into the storeroom with my head bent over, and came out with the sugar. She was still studying me with concern.

I began to invent reasons for going into the house when she was there alone. Using the fire of my imagination I found that I was able to undress her whenever I liked. She grew used to my unnecessary arrivals, and I to her feigned indifference. We hypnotized one another, each looking into the other's eyes. At this point we spoke very little. Our mutual understanding grew, intensified.

One cold night I found my body warming itself beside hers, and she said nothing. We warmed one another and slid on top of each other, face over face, face under face. I slap her cheek to hear the sound it makes. I bite her so her blood will run out. I pretend to stab her, in order to hear the groan I had heard my mother make. And for the first time I understood that girls had something wonderful and delicious, and that, whatever it was, I needed it.

My mother gave birth to a baby. Little sister Khemou was growing big enough to take care of little brother Achor. One evening at the café I was smoking *kif* and getting drunk on wine, sitting outside the door in the fresh air. When my eyes were open I saw the stars in the sky, and when they were shut I saw the stars in my head. The café keeper noticed me sitting there, and said with annoyance: Serve that man a glass of water.

I looked at him dreamily, and in my mind cursed him. The son of a whore! The stars in my head went out. I said: And you? What are you doing here? Give it to him yourself.

He slapped my face. Then he spat at me. I began to laugh without control. One of the *kif*-smokers cried: Can't you see he's *kiffed* and drunk?

That was my last night at the café. I went off into the dark with the night birds whistling in my head, feeling both light and heavy. Walking on the earth was like flying. I was not afraid of the cane-brakes along the road, or of the horrors that might be behind them. In order to feel even drunker I began to sing:

> *Ya Tetuan, ma ahlak*
> *Tol omri ma ninsak*
> *Tol hayatia ahouak.*

I came across a cat, or maybe a rabbit, as I ran in the darkness through the narrow lanes. It could have been a *djinn* pretending to be a cat for all I cared.

About a week after the Aid el Kebir I went with my mother to the stream that ran at the bottom of the orchard. She wanted to wash the hide of the sheep we had sacrificed. Later, when we were at home that night, she exclaimed: Allah! I left the knife down there on the rock. The one I was scraping the sheepskin with.

I said nothing, but ran out through the orchard to the stream. I found the knife, and seized it as if I were going to throw it at an adversary, at the same time glancing across to the other bank of the stream. And I saw a *djinn* advancing towards the water. Like everyone else, I knew that if you see a *djinn*, you must pierce the earth with a steel blade where you stand. With a violent gesture, I threw the knife downward. I tried to run, but my knees failed me. I fell and got up again. I could neither cry out nor turn my head. It seemed to me that if I turned and looked, I would see the monster beside me. I kept slipping and falling and getting up again, until I reached the house, my heart in my throat. As a result I fell ill, got worse, and actually came near to dying. An old man visited the house, a specialist in exorcizing evil spirits from human bodies. The old man accomplished a miracle. He told my mother to sacrifice a black rooster and to carry me seven times around the well in the courtyard. In this way I began after a few days to return to my normal self. When I was well again I told my friends what had happened. All of them believed me implicitly. Both the older and the younger ones knew all about *djenoun*. In those days one thing could all too easily turn into another. Whatever *djinn* might appear, or whatever mere hallucination suggest itself to them, they understood that it came from Allah in direct accordance with their own personal merit or lack of it.

My father now found me a new job in a brick factory, where I earned twenty-five pesetas a week, pushing a wheelbarrow full of clay or bricks back and forth for eight or nine hours a day. At first my hands were covered with blisters. Later the blisters turned into callouses. My face became hard and my body strong.

I left the brick factory and went to work at a pottery kiln. It was the same sort of work, pushing a wheelbarrow, and the work day was just as long, although this time it was I who collected my wages. I gave half to my father in return for my food, lodging and laundry. But I was tired of wheelbarrows. I'm not a donkey, I told my mother when my father could not hear us. Anybody who goes on all his life hauling loads up and down must be a donkey.

And what are you going to do?

I know what I'm going to do, I said.

At lunchtime my father told me: Food costs money in this house. Unless you work, you've got no food or bed here. You understand?

I bowed my head and said: Yes. But inside I said: And you? What do you do? Isn't it my mother who does the work?

I left the kiln and bought the things I needed in order to be a bootblack. I frequented cafés and bars, stood outside doorways, and gathered cigarette butts. I drank the dregs from the wine glasses and ate the *tapas* that were left over on the little plates. The men complained that I gave them a bad shoeshine. It was clear that I had not mastered the craft. Usually the brush fell to the pavement when I changed hands. And the hostility of the other bootblacks bothered me. I became friendly with a newsboy who was about my age. Then I stopped shining shoes and, like him, began to hawk the daily paper *El Diario de Africa*.

# 3

We moved to the quarter called Trancats, and I began to help my mother sell her vegetables and fruit. My work consisted of shouting in a strident voice at the passers-by:

> *¡Vamos a tirar la casa por la ventana!*
> *¡Quien llega tarde no come carne!*
> *¡De balde! ¡De balde vendo hoy!*

Each afternoon I managed secretly to put aside some money with which to buy *majoun* and *kif*. Occasionally I had enough to go to the cinema. One day my friend Tafersiti and I decided to visit a brothel. We drank half a bottle of *mahia* sitting on a wall by the barracks above the Medina.

Lalla Harouda, considered by the boys to be the best whore from whom to learn about sex, came up to us. You've had a lot to drink, haven't you? she said. Tafersiti looked at me. I explained that we were only a little happy. She examined us, an amused expression on her face, and we both were afraid she was not going to let us in.

Well, who's going to go first? she said. I looked at Tafersiti. You go in, he told me.

She wanted the money in advance. I gave it to her without hesitation; it seemed natural that she should have asked for it.

She is selling and I am buying.

She began to take off her clothes, a cigarette hanging from her fleshy lips. The smoke curled upward and made her squint. She turned to me. Open your mouth, she said. She smiled and thrust the cigarette between my lips. Then she turned her back on me, and I unbuttoned her brassiere, my eyes on the sparse hairs in the furrow between her buttocks. She faced me, still smiling, the brassiere dangling from her hand, and took the cigarette from my mouth. I smiled back at her, thinking: She used my lips as an ashtray.

Smoke, she told me. Don't you smoke? Nervously I pulled out a cigarette and lit it. Take off your clothes, she said.

My trousers stood out in front. With agitation I unbuttoned my fly. My heart was pounding. Still no one had a body as beautiful as Asiya or Fatima, but with them it had been only a superficial and slippery contact. This one will let me go into her the way a knife goes into living flesh. I am going to stab what is between her thighs.

She lay back on the bed like a pair of scissors and opened her blades. It was shaved. I remembered Mounat as she crouched and piddled. The legs spread wider now. She seized my sex in her hand.

And suppose it has teeth in it, I thought. I approached her openness with misgivings, then felt the scissors squeezing my legs. She hugged me to her.

You don't even know yet how to get into a woman.

She wet her fingers on her tongue and moved her hand down to the other mouth. Put it in now.

I hesitated.

What's the matter? Go on.

I thought: And if it should have teeth?

Don't be afraid. I'm not going to eat you.

Cautiously I entered her, sinking into her slippery mouth. Sometimes I lost it and could not find it again.

Ay, ay, ay! Not that way!

I remembered my mother telling my father: Not like that! Like this!

So this is the first time you've been with a woman!

I get into her once more. I want her lips and she offers me her cheek. I manage to get hold of her breasts. She objects, and pulls my hand away.

Ah! Ah! Not like that! That's my flesh you're squeezing. You're too young to try that sort of thing. This is your first time.

Fatima is prettier than Lalla Harouda, who won't even let me touch her breasts. She let me have her lips and her breasts too.

The slippery massage by Lalla Harouda did not last very long. Come on, she said. You're through. She pushed me away from her. My sex was still dripping.

Oh, not like that! she cried. You're messing up my bed. Wait. Let me show you.

She spread a handkerchief over her wound. I was thinking of her buttocks. It's true, I said to myself. She's a real professor.

There you are. You've slept with your first woman. Isn't that true? I'm the first, no?

I nodded my head.

You'll always remember me, she told me.

I smiled at her, feeling that she liked me. My snake was still standing. I wanted it to leave its venom inside once again.

Well, what are you waiting for? Wash and put your clothes on. Hurry. Your friend's waiting for his turn.

I put my trousers on. They pushed against my sex. It lay down and then stood up again.

How was it? said Tafersiti.

Wonderful! No teeth!

What? She hasn't any teeth?

I'm not talking about her mouth. Her hole doesn't bite. You'll see. It's warm and soft.

You there! she shouted from the room. Come on inside.

I was thinking: It's not good to look at it, but it feels good. It warms your whole body, and makes you calm and clear-headed. But it's better to do it without looking.

Tafersiti and I would go to the brothel three or four times a week to look for a new woman. Then we would both have her. They all acted more or less the same way in bed: Come on! Hurry up! We went back to the ones who would allow us to fondle their breasts and kiss them, and who would let us take our time.

If they won't let you do that, I told Tafersiti, you're only getting half a piece.

They only let the older ones, he said.

And are we so young?

The women think we are, anyway.

Why don't we go and look at the Spanish women this afternoon?

Good. We'll see what it's like with them.

The first girl we met there would not take us. *Uno solamente*, she insisted. *Nada de dos.*

Only one of us can go, I explained to Tafersiti.

Go in with her, if you want, he told me.

No. We'll both go, or neither one of us.

She can go take a shit, he said.

She's young and pretty.

She can still go and take a shit. In her clothes. There are plenty of others, better than that. You'll see.

I know.

We spoke to another woman, a little older and calmer than the one who had refused us. She wasn't ugly, but the first had been better to look at. What good is beauty, though, if it has pride with it? I thought.

How does she look to you? I asked Tafersiti.

What's the difference? She'll do. The main thing is that she'll take us both.

She's a little fat, I said.

It doesn't matter. We can use her. Afterwards we'll look for something better.

Too much beauty is bad for you, I said.

We tossed a coin to see which one would go first. Tafersiti drew heads. But he said: It would be better if you went first.

You're used to it. You always go first.

I went in. *¡Antonio!* she called. *Trae agua y una toalla.*

A handsome boy came to the doorway, *Ya voy,* he said. His eyelashes had kohl on them, and his face was covered with pink powder. He seemed to have breasts, and they stood out. He wore his trousers very tight.

Give him something, the woman told me. I was confused. I gave him two pesetas. Then I tried to give the woman her fifteen pesetas.

No, no. Afterwards. Are you going to run away, or what? First we make love.

She washed my sex with soap and water. She squeezed it and rolled it. Why is she doing that? I wondered. The Moroccan women don't wash it or squeeze it.

I was unable to keep it from growing hard as she worked, and I was ashamed. She smiled, and I smiled back at her.

*¿Eres fuerte, eh?* she laughed.

She took off her brassiere and underpants. It was not shaved. I expected her to wash herself, too, but she lay back on the bed, one leg across the other, with her hands on her thighs. They all know that the less they show, the more interesting they are, I thought.

So she did not wash. Perhaps that was because she knew she was clean. And now, she did not grip me with her scissors, but merely lay there like a great tuna-fish. I had heard how the Prophet Jonah had been swallowed by a whale. She folded one leg under the other, and I looked between them, thinking that this was a strange position for her to take. But obligingly she let me kiss her lips. They tasted good.

Suddenly she cried: Ay! Ay! Wait! We've got some hairs caught in there. Take it out, and let me move. That wasn't a good way to lie. Perhaps this will be better for you.

She changed her position, and I was afraid she was not going to let me get back in. As far as I was concerned, both positions were good. She did not mind when I touched her breasts, or when I sucked on her lower lip. Filling my mouth with one of her breasts gave me a wild desire to sink my teeth into the flesh. The hairs had caused me some pain as well. She was in no hurry to finish.

How is she? Tafersiti asked when I came out.

Fine! Wonderful! She lets you have everything. She's clean, too, and smells of perfume.

She does?

You'll see for yourself.

That night I dreamed I was sucking a woman's breast. The stream of milk that shot out of it struck me violently in the face.

One day little brother Achor died. His death left me with no feeling of regret. I had heard him crying and seen him crawling, but I had never thought of him as another person.

My new pleasures kept me from being submerged by life at home. Without interest I watched my sister Khemou grow and learn to talk. I was buried in my own melancholy, intent only upon my own body and the pleasure it could give me. Each day the world seemed to become a more complicated place. I slept in the street more often than I slept at home.

My mother lent me some money. Tafersiti and I began to buy fruit and vegetables from the warehouses and sell them for our own profit in the street. When grapes came into season, we bought huge quantities of them and carried them out to sell in the country markets. This did not last very long, and we spent all we had earned in bars and brothels. When winter came we regretted our thoughtlessness.

Khemou had begun to go and sit in the street with my mother as she sold her vegetables, where she could help keep an eye on the small boys who came to steal. One afternoon Comero, the bully of the quarter, slapped her. I was smoking *kif* in a café when a friend came by and told me.

Comero hit your sister. He was trying to steal a head of cabbage. Your mother wasn't there.

I went and found Khemou crying. Some boys I knew came by. He's in the Café Bab et Toute! Why don't you go and beat him up? You can do it. I know you can. Boras butted him in the face and knocked him out. Yes! Fight him! We're all with you. He'll have nobody on his side. Who's as good as you with a razor-blade?

I bought three razor-blades and sent friends to tell Comero I would be waiting for him outside the walls. We began in the Souq el Berra with our fists. He was stronger than I was, but I managed to keep out of his reach. When I saw that he was going to win, I pulled out one of the razor-blades and began to slash his face and hands and chest. My friends and I ran off, leaving him yelling and dancing in circles.

My father's brothers had left the Rif and gone to Oran to live, and he had been preparing to go and see them. That night, having learned of the fight, he called in some of the neighbours and got them to help him catch me. He had been going to make the trip by himself, but now he went and bought another ticket, and at one in the morning he and I boarded a bus for Nador. We got down at Ketama for some black coffee. It was the first time I had walked on snow. The voyage was tiring. We ate dry bread and hard-boiled eggs, and we crossed the River Moulouya on the shoulders of the men who always waited there to help those who did not want to face the police on the bridge. Then we walked on to a place in the road further ahead, and bought a ride on a truck going past.

We passed a night in Oujda at the house of some friends of my father's. I spent the next morning killing the lice that crawled everywhere in my clothing.

# 4

It was night when we arrived in Oran. My father found a man who spoke Riffian, and he showed us to the house in the New Medina where my father's friends lived. There the houses were built into the cliffs like caves, and dogs ran out at us, barking. One of them tore my trousers. I was walking ahead of my father while he picked up stones to throw at them. When they came nearer, he clubbed them with the stick he was carrying. He swore at the dogs and then he swore at me. Go on ahead, you coward, damn you!

I stumbled and fell. He pounded me with the stick, and I yelled. As I continued to walk ahead, he prodded me in the back. The stones under my feet were pointed, and I was walking through nettles. He hits me and curses me aloud, and I do the same to him secretly. Without my imagination I should have exploded.

A man in tattered clothing came out of one of the caves and greeted us. We went inside. His wife was on the floor praying, dressed in spotless white.

Presently the woman asked me for news of my mother and my brothers and sisters who had been born in exile, in Tangier. The only one she had seen was Abdelqader, and she was sad to hear of his death. I did not tell her how he had died. The last time I saw you, you were only five or six years old, she told me. And here it is nine years later.

The following day we met my uncle and my grandmother in Douar ej Jdid, and then we went to see my aunt in the quarter of Serimine. She had married a man from Marrakech.

You've grown up, my grandmother told me. Soon you'll be a man. Then you'll work and help me to live. Isn't that right?

Yes. She was thin and sick.

My father left me behind with my aunt, and went on to look for his brothers in other Algerian cities far from Oran. Three months later a letter came from him saying that he had gone back to Tetuan, and that it would be better for me to stay on in Oran.

My aunt got her husband to find me a job, and soon I was working on the farm of the same French woman in whose stable he worked. I was in the vineyard from five in the morning to six in the evening. The pause at midday for eating and resting lasted only an hour, but often we managed to prolong it another hour more, if nobody came by. My work consisted in guiding two mules along the ploughed tracks in the earth.

I grew tanned, and the palms of my hand became calloused. The old farm labourer under whom I worked treated me according to the way he felt at the moment. Depending on the circumstances he could be kind or heartless. I learned that his harsh words were only a way of expressing the frustration he felt at the work he was forced to do. What hurt me in his behaviour was the fact that he treated me as a peasant.

The country you come from has produced only one man, and that was Abd el Krim el Khattabi, he would tell me.

I had not yet heard of Abd el Krim, and had no idea who he was.

I continued this backbreaking work for six months. On Sundays I would go out to catch birds, or walk to the city. One day I tried in vain to climb a high tree. That leg was tall and smooth. I grew very angry at being repulsed, and so I went to the shed and filled a can with gasoline. I doused the tree trunk and lit a match. The flames were beautiful. I said to the charred tree: Now you're not so smooth. I can climb you, as high as I want.

There was no one in sight. The place was hidden from the farmhouse and its outbuildings. The tree looked like a woman, only it was without legs, and its branches took the place of a head.

I looked for a smaller tree, and found it, smooth and bright. I discovered that when I put my arms around it, they met at the back. I cut the outline of a woman on the trunk, with head and torso, and then I began the creation. For a full week I was busy cutting out two deep holes for the breasts, as well as another even deeper one at the meeting of the legs. And so I made the tree woman. Whenever I wanted to amuse myself I fastened an orange into each breast-hole, and sucked on them. Sometimes I substituted apples, so that I could chew pieces out of them. The opening between the thighs had to be lubricated, and then I was able to transfer all the images in my memory to the tree woman.

One evening my aunt's husband told me: Tomorrow you won't be going to the vineyard. Madame Segundi, the foreman's wife, wants to see you. She may let you work for her in the house. That depends on whether she likes you.

I was overjoyed. But I was troubled by his final words: If she likes you.

Madame Segundi was friendly and pleasant. She was also young and attractive, and the litheness of her body reminded me of Asiya. Sitting facing her I was humble, even timid. But it was not so in my fantasies. She would be a marvellous new toy for my dreams; it is best to change one's dreams each day. She spoke to me in Spanish, and I tried desperately to remember the few words I still knew.

Madame Segundi gave me three days in which to prepare myself for work. I spent them at the circus, the cinema, and the cafés. I carried a bottle of wine with me wherever I went. At night I would drink it at the farm in the small hut that stood alongside my uncle's house. The only one to witness my nocturnal pleasures was Tigre, the dog.

My pretty mistress taught me how to wash dishes and dry them, and how to fry eggs and fish. One day I cooked her a Moroccan *tajine*, and she was delighted with it. She got into the habit of asking for it each week. Today we'll have your Moroccan food. But you've got to make it by yourself.

I enjoyed working for her, and I used her as a dream object whenever I felt excited. I had begun to miss the whores of Tetuan. Slow or fast, kissing lips and breasts, or only the cheeks, neck and shoulders, it did not matter. But in Oran, although I had heard about them, I had no idea how to find the brothels. Even if I had known where they were, I could not have gone alone. I should have needed a friend to take me. The friends I had there in Oran were all very serious-minded. It would have been unthinkable for me to mention my desires to anyone at the farm. How could I have brought up the subject, when not one of them ever smiled? Sometimes I watched Monsieur Segundi kiss his beautiful wife and lightly run his hands over her body. He did not mind doing it in front of me. Usually I served them their breakfast in bed, he bare-chested, and she in her transparent nightgown that showed her nipples, like two raisins, underneath. Even to think of the space between them filled my mouth with saliva and made my senses begin to blur.

One day she asked me to wash her husband's underwear. As I plunged the garments into the water I thought: What is this? One man shouldn't be washing another man's underwear. Then I said to Monique, my mistress: No. I'm not going to wash these clothes.

Why not?

These are Monsieur Segundi's shorts.

And so?

I hung my head and said: A man doesn't wash another man's underwear.

She laughed. And what about women's underwear?

I hesitated, and then told her: Women's clothes are different. A man can wash them for her if she can't do it herself.

You're very funny, she said. You're marvellous! Is that the custom in Morocco?

I was not certain whether it was a true custom, or only one which I had just invented. There was no precedent for it in my experience. But I said: Yes. That's our custom in Morocco.

It's very strange, she said.

They laughed together about it, she and her husband. A few days later it was Monsieur Segundi himself who ordered me to wash his underpants. I said no. He insisted, and I continued to refuse.

What do you mean, you won't wash them? he demanded.

That's what I mean.

Then go home and stay there!

Three days later I was sent back to work by my relatives, who had the Segundis' approval. My mistress's parents came from Sidi bel Abbès to visit her, and her father talked with me about his Spanish origins. He pitied me, he said, for not being able to read or write in any language, and he asked me if they did not teach either Arabic or Spanish in Tetuan.

Yes, I've heard they teach both Arabic and Spanish, I said.

They why didn't you go to school?

Because my father never thought of sending me.

Was it that he didn't send you, or that you didn't want to go?

I don't know, I said. But he didn't ever take me to any school.

He looked for a moment at my forehead. How did you get that scar?

I was crossing the street and there was a bicycle race going on, I told him.

I wondered later why some men were so much nicer than my father.

The summer afternoons in Oran are fine and long. The old men play checkers. The young ones fence with wooden swords. The women are inside, or talking in their doorways. The children are everywhere, playing games and fashioning toys out of clay and pieces of wood or cane.

I went to Sidi bel Abbès with my employers. All the members of Madame Segundi's family were good to me, but it was her father who seemed particularly to like me. I took a walk in the town. It was sad and sinister, although I liked the main avenue and the cathedral. I heard a lot of Spanish being spoken in the streets. People passed by me on all sides, but there was no question of speaking to any of them, nor did they speak to me. I was among them, but far from them. I came to a street fair. The circus spectacle began at five, and so I could not see it. I had to be back at the Segundis' house before that. I smoked one cigarette after the other, and drank two glasses of wine in a Spanish bar. Then I went to look at the circus animals in their cages. I stopped in front of a monkey. There were some children beside its cage, and they were teasing it. I have no idea how it happened, but suddenly I felt the monkey's claws tearing my face. I yelled and jumped back. The guard came and chased the children away. Then he looked at my scratches and patted my shoulder, shouting again at the fleeing children.

I saw something which made me forget the pain in my face for a moment: a young couple embracing behind the circus tent, all shining in their satin costumes. Watching their kisses awoke all my senses. I thought how wonderful circus life must be. And I remembered the orchard at Aïn Khabbès, Asiya undressing, I sliding on Fatima's naked body, and the whores at the brothel in Tetuan who had opened their thighs to me.

When I got back to the house they painted my face with iodine. They seemed to think the scratches were important. Madame Segundi's aunt took care of me, and let me go for a walk in her garden. Spiders' webs covered all the plants. Under the dome of the summerhouse I noticed two dusty wooden benches half eaten away by termites. The sight filled me with profound melancholy. The garden was lugubrious. Pieces of broken objects were scattered here and there among the plants. From time to time in the trees above a bird sang briefly or fluttered its wings. Lime spattered on my head and shoulders.

We drove back to Oran. The next day the scratches on my face had turned black. When Sunday came, my employers did not take me with them when they went for their usual ride. I stayed behind alone in the house.

I turned on the radio for a moment. Then I shut it off and began to play the phonograph. I did not understand the words being sung on the records, but the music and the voices took me off to a world that I saw all in bluish-green. My mistress Monique knew I liked 'The Blue Danube'. When she is feeling in unusually good spirits she will say: I'm going to put on your record.

I took up the photograph album and looked through the family pictures. There were some snapshots of Monique when she was a little girl. I spoke to them: Grow up! Grow up right away! As I turned the pages, she did grow up. I studied the pictures taken at the beach, where she was coming out of the water, or lying on the sand with her husband, or alone. There are three colour photographs of her where she is completely naked. In the first she is standing, leaning forward a little, with her hands folded below her belly. In the next she is kneeling on a fur-covered divan, bust erect, arms straight out behind her. I imagined her asking me: Do you like this pose? And I answered: Beautiful! Marvellous! In the third picture she is lying back on the couch, her hands behind her head, one leg slightly turned outward. Come on, said the picture. You're mine, I told the silent woman, and I wondered who could have taken such pictures of her. Her husband, probably. If I had had a camera that morning long ago, I could have photographed Asiya coming towards the tank, bathing naked, searching frantically for her pyjamas, and running away through the orchard in fright.

I went down into the food cellar to celebrate the imaginary nuptials. First I opened the tap of a barrel and filled a carafe with red wine whose taste I knew and liked. I put some olives and some Danish Blue cheese on a plate. Then I ate and drank slowly. Certain images from the time of Aïn Khabbès activated my memory. From one of the photographs the lovely Monique was winking at me. I blew some life into it, and she stretched. She is enjoying herself now with her husband. I got a cake of hand soap and a glass of warm water from the bathroom. The photograph set off the thrill of excitement that was necessary for the delicious dream to commence. I could not have said whether I was imagining the photograph, or whether it had invented me. The delight in my body increases. I begin the dragon's massage. It swells and reddens, and lifts its head. It sweats and pants, and I taste honey. Colours take over, one slipping after the other, drowning itself in the other, each changing into another, without colour, or the colour of all colours. I no longer knew where I was.

I heard footsteps. Rapidly I closed my fly.

What are you doing here? she demanded.

Tell me. What are you doing down here? And with my photograph album! What are you doing with that?

She seized the album and started up the stairs. I followed, hanging my head.

Who gave you permission to take my photograph album? Tell me that.

She slapped me. The blow brought about the culmination of my pleasure.

You're drunk. You've been drinking, haven't you? I forbid you ever to do such a thing again.

I wandered in a blind rage across the fields. Tigre ran along with me, sometimes behind, sometimes ahead of me. I suddenly remembered that I had left the cake of soap and the glass of water in the cellar. Monique will think: And he uses my soap, too. I felt myself drowning in shame. Now she'll know I make love with her by myself.

On my return to the farm I found all the workmen with their families, standing in a circle around a group of sheep that had been hit by a train. Some of them had still been alive, and they had had their throats cut according to holy law. The ones already dead were of no use. That night the jackals howled and yapped close to the house. They're eating the insides now,

I thought. If I had been one of those sheep, they'd be ripping my belly now with their fangs.

Tigre came in, blood bubbling out of him, and began to run in a circle. Then he runs out and back in, whining the whole time. He is trying to lick the wounds on his neck. I went to my aunt's house and woke her. She put ashes on him and bandaged him. The bites are deep, she said. Five or six jackals must have attacked him at once.

I tied Tigre up in my cabin for fear he would run out again, and I watched him die, little by little. He was dead before I went to sleep.

In the morning I put his body into a wheelbarrow and carted it a long way out into the country, where I buried it beside an olive tree. This was the first time I had buried a dead body. It gave me a strange feeling. I began to ask myself: Why did this dog have to die in such a painful way? And I thought of the sheep that had been mangled by the train. The shepherd is stupid. Tigre is stupid. If he had known what death was, he wouldn't have died like this. But the world is full of stupidity. I am stupid too.

That day when I buried Tigre, I did not want to go to the main house and see Madame Segundi. I was still ashamed to face her. If you know what's good for you, said my aunt, you'll go and see your mistress. You're supposed to be working.

Monique herself came to see my aunt, and sat down. I began to translate what one of them said to the other. My aunt knew only Riffian and Arabic. She used Riffian now, and Monique used Spanish. She was lovely and full of charm that afternoon. Women are difficult to understand. When a man is sure he is going to have trouble with a woman, it often turns out that he is wrong. And when he thinks a woman has forgiven him, he may be going straight towards the trouble he originally expected. Salvation and disaster depend upon the way she happens to feel at the moment. I sensed that Monique did not blame me for what I had done, but neither could she let it pass unnoticed. And so she asked me: Are you sick?

No, I'm not sick.

Then why didn't you come to work today?

I did not answer. Then I said: The jackals killed Tigre last night.

Your uncle told me. Poor dog! He was good and strong. Where did you bury him?

Under an olive tree.

Your uncle will find another dog. She got up and took my hand. Her goodwill made me even more ashamed. *Allez!* Come to the house with me, she said.

Then she hasn't told her husband, I thought. Perhaps she was ashamed to.

I had often dreamed of being able to fly. Likewise I had dreamed of being in a cave strewn with lengths of silk and rugs, and where the walls were painted with brilliant designs. I had only to make a gesture, and a platter would be there, bearing whatever it was that I felt like eating. If I clapped my hands, a marvellous girl would appear, one who had never been touched by a man, to dance naked in a fog of incense smoke before me.

One morning after her husband had gone out, I saw Monique go into the bathroom with a packet of cotton and a pair of her underpants. In the garbage pail I had often seen wads of cotton soaked with dark blood. I wondered where the blood came from.

I walked carefully over to the door and peeked through the keyhole. She takes off the underwear she has on and sits down on the bidet. She makes water. Then she washes between her legs. She pats a small towel into her wound, like the first woman I ever slept with in the brothel in Tetuan. She seizes a handful of absorbent cotton, pulls out the towel and examines it, and throws it into the bathtub. Then she puts the cotton into the wound and pulls on the clean underpants. I wondered if all women bled like this one, like pretty Monique. If they bleed all the time, it's disgusting.

There was a boy who lived nearby, a little younger than I. One day we took a walk into the country. I told him we were going to catch birds in the traps we carried with us. The boy was handsome, and delicate as a girl. He wore shorts that came above his knees. We ate meat and hard-boiled eggs under the olive trees. Then I persuaded him to smoke a cigarette and drink a little wine. He coughed when he tried to inhale the smoke, and after he had drunk from the bottle he shuddered. This is the first time I've smoked or drunk wine, he said, and I told him what they had told me in Tetuan: You won't cough or make faces the next time. That happens only the first time. It was the same way with me.

Do you feel sick? I asked him.

Just a little.

We walked into a field of wheat. To be drunk is relaxing. His cheeks are pink, his lips bright red. We sat down in the middle of the wheat, and I lay back. He did likewise. I thought of Tetuan, of a song that began: *I loved a girl in Andalucia. She was young, she was tiny, she was tanned.*

The wine ran through me, and I found myself trembling. My hand stroked his. He pulled away and sat up, looking at me with an expression of fear. What do you want? he demanded.

Nothing. What's the matter? Lie down. I was joking.

I don't like that sort of joke.

With my eyes I said: I do, with you.

He made as if to rise. I seized his hand. I was still trembling. He wrenched his hand away and got to his feet. Before he could take his first step, I wrapped my arms around his legs, so that he fell. I fell partially on top of him.

I'm going to tell my mother! he cried. And my father too!

First he bites my hand, and then he bites the earth.

That night my aunt scolded me. I was mortified, and denied everything. I swore I had done nothing to him. Later I saw her kissing the boy's mother on the top of her head, begging her pardon. I was ashamed.

Your mother must have suffered when you lived in Tetuan, she told me. If you go on like this, your whole family will suffer, and so will you. Behave yourself.

I imagined saying to her: What should I do to behave myself, aunt? How?

And I imagined her answering: Don't do things you know are wrong.

Then I would have said: But I have to. I like everything that's wrong. Those are the best things.

I don't understand you.

I don't understand myself.

Madame Segundi began to notice my preoccupied expression and the slowing down in the tempo of my work. You miss your family in Tetuan, she said.

I don't know.

Listen. We're going to give you a whole month's vacation. A month is enough for you to go and visit your family, and get back here.

I agreed to go to Tetuan and return. I saw my grandmother and my uncle very seldom. Sometimes when they came to the farm to visit my aunt, I was not there. I felt no particular fondness for them, neither affection nor dislike.

The only time Oran looked pleasant to me was the day I left. There is a saying that goes:

> *Ed dakhel en Oueheran zerbanne,*
> *Ou el harej menha harbanne.*

On the way back to Tetuan I tried to decide which was better. Oran is exile and Tetuan is imprisonment. And since I am happier in Tetuan than in Oran, that means I prefer jail in my native land to freedom in exile.

I spent two days in Melilla and one in Nador. I talked about Oran with people I did not know. One of them said: With everybody trying to get to Oran, here you are coming away from it!

# 5

Once I found myself back in Tetuan, I was sure that I should not be returning to Oran. My mother had given birth to another girl, but the baby had died almost at birth. Now her belly was very full again. My father was still happily unemployed. He spent the greater part of his day in the Feddane talking to madmen and friends who had been wounded in the Spanish Civil War. My sister Khemou went on growing, and my mother already relied upon her help at the vegetable stand. Some friends arranged a reconciliation between Comero and me. He now had a scar that ran right along his cheek. At the brothel I found that some of the girls were gone and new ones had taken their place. Because I enjoyed it, I formed the habit of sleeping in the alleys along with the other vagabonds. One morning as I lay asleep in the street a girl woke me up and asked me if I were not the son of Sida Maimouna. I said I was.

Why don't you sleep at home, then?

My father threw me out.

The girl was lame. She went and got me a piece of buttered bread and a glass of coffee. I should have been ashamed to refuse her generosity. However, I resolved to get up earlier in the future. I was beginning to distrust people who showed goodwill towards me, whether they were men or women.

I returned to the bakery where I had so often slept in the past, where I would roll myself up like a hedgehog, my back pushed against the warm oven. Whenever I move in the night, or get up to go out and relieve myself, I find several cats asleep on top of me. Often I enjoyed the sound of their purring. It reminded me of a motor going in a distant factory. I loved muted sounds, whether they came from far or near. The songs from the cafés, heard from far away, were beautifully sad.

Another morning it was a man who woke me up. Aren't you the son of Si Haddou?

No, I'm not.

He insisted. Aren't you his son Mohamed?

No. I'm not his son.

Then what is your name?

Mohamed.

But your father is Si Haddou Allal Choukri. And your mother is Sida Maimouna.

I told you no.

Who is your father, then?

He's dead. He died a long time ago.

And what was his name?

I don't know.

You don't know the name of your own father?

I did know it, but I've forgotten. I was still in my mother's belly when he died.

He looked at me a moment, and then said: It looks to me as if there's something the matter with your brain.

He held out two pesetas. Here. You must be hungry. Go and buy yourself some breakfast.

I don't need anything, I said curtly. I have money.

He seemed mystified. I don't understand. You have money, and you sleep here in the corner like a cat. You're a little crazy.

I was angry. The cat is you, and you're completely crazy! Suddenly I howled into his face, like a wolf. *Aaaaooou!* Then I walked away, leaving him standing there, saying: *Bismillah rahman er rahim!* Preserve me from the young ones of today!

My mother now gave birth to another girl, whom she named Zohra, after the one who had just died. A rat bit her on the hand one night, and she died, too.

My father had a habit of stealing up behind me in the street and seizing my shirt collar. Then with one hand he would twist my arm behind my back, while with the other he would beat me until the blood ran. When that happened, I knew the thick military belt was waiting at home for me. And when his arms and legs were tired from beating and kicking, he would bite my shoulders and arms, pinch my ears, and buffet my face with his fists. If he catches me in the street, someone usually intervenes and sets me free. But he has learned not to do it in the street. So now, when he grabs me I fall to the pavement and yell as loud as I can. He will sweep the pavement with me for a moment, kicking me all the while, until I manage to get out of his grip and go far enough away from him to be able to curse him.

One morning I sat in a café smoking *kif* with two pickpockets. We decided to work together that day in order to spend a night of debauchery at the brothel. We went to the Plaza Nueva where the crowd was densest. It was not long before I felt the furious grip of my father's hand on the back of my neck. Before I had time to throw myself down, my two companions had gone at him with their fists and heads. I heard him shouting for help between groans. As I looked back at him, I saw that he had both hands over his face, and blood was trickling rapidly between his fingers.

What was the matter with that son of a bitch? Abdeslam demanded.

Nothing, I said. That was my father.

Your father!

Sebtaoui came up then, exclaiming:

Son of garbage! Son of a whore! What did he want with you?

It was his father.

His father! He turned to me.

Yes, my father. But you should have hit him harder. He's a pig.

When we got to the end of the alley at Et Talaa, I saw a drunk coming out of a house. It was a cold rainy night.

The rain will cut down the cold, said Abdeslam.

The drunk staggered past us. We heard a thud. He's very drunk, Sebtaoui said. Then we saw the man struggling to get up. We went on to the same doorway he had come out of. A woman appeared, her breath stinking of alcohol, and showed us into the house. She took Abdeslam's head between her hands and kissed him on the lips, slowly and noisily.

What did you bring me today? she began. What have you brought for your mother?

Anything, he told her. Whatever you want.

Sebtaoui walked into a brightly lit room from which came the sound of talking and laughter.

Abdeslam introduced me to the drunken woman. Mama, he said, this is a new friend.

She looked at me between half-shut lids.

He's going to stay up with us tonight, he went on.

She took my head between her hands gently, and kissed my lips, making a smacking sound. You're welcome in our house, she said, still touching my face, tilting her head back slightly and looking squarely into my eyes. What does this woman want of me? I wondered. Is she trying to put a spell on me, perhaps?

Abdeslam watched his mother, smiling. But is she really his mother? Or is he having fun with me? Perhaps she only brought him up.

Everybody go upstairs, she said.

Sebtaoui and I climbed the stairs to the floor above, leaving Abdeslam talking to his mother. A small girl came in carrying a tray. She placed a bottle of cognac on it, and went out. Nothing better than cognac on a cold night like this, said Sebtaoui.

That's right, I said.

We had had a delicious dinner. The purse we had finally

succeeded in stealing (thanks to a system whereby Sebtaoui opened the foreign woman's handbag, Abdeslam reached in and removed the purse, and I was left with it) proved to have in it more than three thousand pesetas.

What's happened to Abdeslam? I said finally.

He's getting his mother to send out for three girls. A lot of them don't whore publicly. They stay home and wait for the madame to get in touch with them. Some of them are married. Once in a while you'll even find a virgin.

How can you sleep with a girl who's still a virgin?

You can't. She just comes along with the other girls. When it's time to sleep, the madame either sends somebody along with the girl to see that she gets home, or lets her spend the night with her.

And suppose somebody wants a virgin? I said.

In that case, he pays what it costs.

How much, for instance?

He looked at me. Is that what you want? Do you want to break in a virgin?

No, I was just wondering.

You'd have to pay at least a thousand or fifteen hundred pesetas.

Doesn't Abdeslam's mother have any girls here in the house? I asked him. I thought I heard some girls talking in that room you went into.

She's got two professionals here, yes, he said. They're very pretty, too. But Abdeslam and I are fed up with them. There are other good ones who come once in a while. Tonight there's only one outside girl down there, and she's drinking cognac as fast as she can, to kill the pain in her tooth.

We heard the voices and laughter of girls from below. Here they are, said Sebtaoui. They're coming up.

Abdeslam's mother appeared, wreathed in smiles, and behind her came three girls wearing caftans. It's a real wedding, I thought to myself.

The woman poured herself a glass of cognac and went out. Abdeslam brought in a carton of Virginia cigarettes. With no hesitating the girls sat down, one beside each of us. That was the first night.

For three days I did not go out into the street. Each morning the girls walked to the *hammam* to bathe. They would come back in the afternoon, clean, perfumed and painted. Sebtaoui and Abdeslam go out together. I prefer to stay in, asleep, or daydreaming, recalling scenes from Tangier, Tetuan or Oran. At night, life took on the flavour of eternity. In the three days I spent only three hundred pesetas. Sometimes Sida Aziza, Abdeslam's mother, comes in to see me, to talk and drink and chainsmoke Virginia cigarettes, or even *kif*.

The fourth evening neither Abdeslam nor Sebtaoui came back, and Sida Aziza sent me out to look for them. Two hours later I returned, having failed to find them, and Sida Aziza sobbed when she saw me. They've been arrested, she declared. I had no idea of how to calm her. Now and then I murmured: I hope they haven't caught them.

I thought of the things that could happen to my two companions. Sida Aziza came and went, back and forth, always carrying a full glass in her hand, until one in the morning. Sometimes she was sobbing, and sometimes laughing.

There's a girl downstairs who's going to sleep by herself. Do you want to sleep with her? Don't give her anything. I'll fix it up with her later.

I smiled. She drained her glass at one gulp, and said: You remind me of my brother Salam who died when he was about your age. He got hit by a car.

She refilled her glass, walked out of the room, and began to call: Yasmina! Come up!

I heard the two of them whispering outside the door, and I thought: She's arranging it for me. The girl came in, smiling modestly. She wore a caftan and her perfume was strong.

It's still very cold out, in spite of all the rain that's fallen, she said. I mixed her cognac with *limonada*. We did not say very much. Her presence was an antidote to my boredom. I took her hand in mine, and said with my eyes and my smile:

There are a lot of things I don't understand. And you, Yasmina?

The same with me. There are many things I don't understand either, her eyes seemed to say.

# 6

It was the neighbours who forced a truce between my father and me. I went back to helping my mother run her vegetable stand. But I was forbidden to go out at night, which was unbearable. Nights were all I had, since I spent the entire day in the street with my mother.

One morning two secret policemen stood beside the vegetable stand: a Moroccan and a Spaniard. Come with us, said the Moroccan. I thought then of Abdeslam and Sebtaoui. Across from our stall Lalla Kinza sold mint. Her son was there. I asked him to mind the stall for me until I got back, or until my mother returned from the market.

They took me to the *jefatura*. Where are Abdeslam and Sebtaoui? the Moroccan asked me.

I don't know them.

What do you mean, you don't know them?

That's right.

He slapped me twice and seized the front of my clothing with one hand, twisting it around. Listen! If you don't tell us the truth, we're going to put your face on the back of your head. You understand?

A Spanish policeman put his head out of an office and said: Take him to Señor Alvarez.

He was looking down when I went in. Then he slowly

raised his head. Aha! So it's you!

I remembered Aïn Khabbès. In the old days I gave his son Julio all the birds that had died in my traps, because they were not edible. And his wife used to send me to the *baqal* or take me to market with her to help carry the food back to her house.

Where does your family live now? he asked me.

In Trancats.

Does your mother still sell vegetables?

Yes.

And you. What do you do?

I help her at the stand.

But you also go out with certain pickpockets.

No! I don't know any thieves.

Don't you know Abdeslam and Sebtaoui?

Sometimes I see them at the Café Trancats, but I don't go out with them.

Have you any idea where they might be?

I don't know.

How long is it since you saw them?

More than a week.

He looked down briefly at the papers on his desk. Ayayay! he exclaimed. After a moment, he said: All right. You can go. But be careful you don't get caught with thieves some day.

I thanked him and went out. In the street I began to spit out the flecks of blood that I had been swallowing while I was in the presence of Señor Alba. (That was the name we used to give him in the old days.) I was thinking: If there's anybody in the world I wish would die before his hour comes, it's my father. And if there were others, they would surely look like him. How many times have I killed him in my mind? All that's needed is for me really to kill him.

I refused to eat the meal, although it tempted me. I did not want to be late to the cinema. I had decided to eat chicken and peas in my imagination that evening. My hand always shakes when I cut a piece of meat in front of him. He glares at me, so that I eat distractedly, like a nervous cat. His essence stays with us even when he is not there himself. None of us had the right to touch anything. His will was necessarily our choice. Sometimes I ask for my share of the food earlier, so that I can eat it by myself. But my mother tells me: No. You shouldn't eat alone. It's a bad habit.

My father is closer to Allah than we are, and nearer to the prophets and saints. Many times I have imagined being able to eat in peace, and all I wanted. His presence makes me doubt the reality of whatever food is offered me. My mother tells me: Your father's not going to eat with us today. Sit down at the *taifor* with us and eat.

I don't want anything.

He is not at home but he is here because I'm afraid of him.

Mohamed! Sit down with us and eat, I tell you!

No! I shout. I'm not going to eat.

Why not?

I've already eaten chicken with onions, raisins and almonds.

Where? she demanded.

I tapped my forehead. Here, I told her.

Are you crazy, or what?

I told you, I'm full. You understand?

Don't let him come in later and find you eating by yourself.

Thus she holds him over my head when she wants her own way. My glance upwards at her was dictated by my fear. I began to eat without appetite. My love for her is bound up with my hatred for him. I ceased to eat. He came in. Now the fear is really with me. An instant ago I was imagining his existence. But now here he is, as real as the dish of repulsive tripe on the *taifor*.

Why aren't you eating?

I'm full, I told him.

It's a lie. You're not full. Not to my way of thinking.

I swear I can't eat any more.

You're lying. I know you. You're the son of this whore here.

I've been a whore only with you, she told him. People would know about it if I'd been a whore.

He hit her in the face.

You always humiliate me like this, she cried defiantly.

He hit her a second time, and bellowed at her and at Khemou: Stop eating, you two! Then he turned back to me. You're going to eat it all by yourself. Just you. He's going to eat it all, and with no help. By himself! You're going to eat it, I tell you. Did you hear me or not?

So that he will not hit me, I say: Yes.

Well, get busy. What are you waiting for?

No! No! cried my mother. You're going to kill him!

Shut up! What a whore she is! Let him die. After he's gone, you can follow him.

She knelt, raising her face to his. He faces her, like a giant looking down at a midget. The flock is his. He can begin with whichever one he wants. Her resistance has dissolved into sobs. Khemou is all bent over, and I can see her trembling.

By himself! Come on! Start! I'll show you how to eat. From now on you're not going to refuse anything that's offered you. Do you hear?

I looked back at him with tempered revolt on my face.

Don't look at me that way! He slapped me with all his strength. I hung my head. With the tip of my tongue I felt along the inside of my lower lip. There was a painful cut.

You won't even refuse carrion if it's given you!

My mouth is slowly filling with liquid, warm, salty, sweet, delicious. I can feel my stomach swelling. With all my willpower I forced myself to believe that this was a bet, and that I had to win it.

Chewing was a bloody, salty operation. Each mouthful deepens the hatred. Why am I always with this man, simply because he happens to be my father? If I were stronger than he, he would be sitting here in my place eating. I'd be just as hard and crazy as he is.

I awoke in the Hospital Nacional, breathing slowly. They had

66

pumped my stomach. I could still feel the cramps.

His voice reminds me of the needle going into the flesh when the injection is badly given.

Her voice: Asleep.

He's got to eat with us.

He's tired. He's been working very hard with me at the stall.

She puts him off. Which is why I do not hate her as I do him, or wish for her death as I do for his. When he comes into the house, only he has the right to exist.

Sometimes I make mistakes. I heard him talking, thought there was someone with him, went upstairs, and was surprised. I could not go back. I found him sitting alone, an ominous expression on his face. He frowned when he saw me. He had been cursing us who were not present, and thus we were all there around him. He drags back those who are not here, and pronounces judgement on them. Whatever he pleases. Like Allah.

Where's your mother?

Buying vegetables. At the wholesale market.

Who's at the stall?

Khemou.

And you?

Mother didn't want me to go with her.

And now you've come here to eat?

No.

Come on. You thought I'd gone to the Feddane. I know a little about you, when you come in and go out, you son of a bitch. Tell me. Isn't that true? Speak up. I don't feel like your father. Who knows? Maybe somebody else was with your mother. You're nothing like me. More like her. She spoils you the whole time. You plot together against me. You defend each other. You never listen to what I tell you. Isn't it true, what I'm saying? Speak up, you damned whelp! You hate me so much you wish I were dead.

I thought to myself: Now you're beginning to make sense.

You want her all to yourself. She's the only thing in the

world you care about.

That's true, I thought. You don't think I'm going to love a dog like you!

I can see the love in her eyes, and in yours too. Anybody'd think you were still sucking her milk.

And you? I thought. I wonder how your mother was with you.

You've still got her milk in you. But I'm the one who married her. She's your mother, yes. But I'm your father. If there's anybody you should listen to, it's me. Nobody else, just me! Me alone! You obey me, not her, do you hear?

I hear you perfectly, O Khalifa of Allah on earth, I said without speaking.

But it's no good talking to you, he went on. Words don't mean anything. Even when I'm in front of you, you don't believe I'm here. I want every one of my children to think of me as always in front of him, whether I'm here or not. Do you hear me, damn you?

I hear, O messenger of Allah!

The only thing you're good for is to bite your mother's nipples.

I remained present in front of him as he wanted me to.

Tell me. Just why did you come here now?

Mother told me to come home.

Why?

To clean the room.

You're all alike, you liars. She doesn't dare to leave you at the stall because you steal the money. She doesn't take you with her to the market because you eat everything in sight. The vegetable men and the porters down there have told me all about you. They've caught you in the act. Filling your pockets with fruit and nuts, and insulting them if they say anything. If only I could find a way to get rid of you once and for all, damn you!

That's just how I feel, too, I said silently to the maniac.

I wish I knew why I hate you so much, he went on. Now go out to the stall. Don't let the kids steal from Khemou.

I was trembling as I went back down the stairs. I don't want to be late to the cinema.

He's tired. He's been working very hard with me at the stall. She puts him off. Which is why I do not hate her as I do him.

I tiptoe carefully up to the roof. He is quiet now because he is filling his mouth. He eats like an animal. I tie the rope with which I am going to escape, and look behind me. His ghost is standing there.

Where are you going, damn you? Stay where you are.

Without hesitation I leapt out and caught hold of the thick electric cables that were strung along the street. I heard him yelling. His hands reach out into the emptiness to strangle me. I thought to myself: I knew all along this was going to happen. My intuition didn't play me false.

You wait, you son of a whore!

Then he was not there. I looked down. It made me a little dizzy.

He'll go out of the house and try to catch me as I fall, I thought. Then he'll grind me to a pulp. He's very bad tonight.

I breathed deeply, shut my eyes, and let myself drop, landing on top of a pile of stones and rubbish. As I ran my foot hit something alive and round.

My head! Who's that? Grab him! Stop thief! Help!

Everything rolls and slides under my bare feet. I can tell the difference between melons or water-melons and human heads only when I hear someone cry out under my feet.

The night-watchman came towards me. Hey, you! Stop! Come here! The old Spaniard danced about as he shook his club at me. Come here, boy! Come here, damn you!

I turned to the left, hearing the watchman's whistle. Someone's ghost was running desperately behind me. Five or six figures moved in the background, gesticulating and pointing. I could hear their faint cries in the quiet street. I slowed down, but I was afraid one of them might take another alley, cut me off, and be standing there ahead of me, waiting. And it might be my accursed father. Again I began to run as fast as I could. I'll keep running until I fall, I thought. Until I drop like a balloon that's had a pin stuck into it.

In the cinema I lit a cigarette. From time to time I rubbed my bleeding feet with the tips of my fingers. I imagined my father coming towards me to seize my neck with his two powerful hands. He has become the villain in the film. As if I were breaking a feather between my fingers, I pulled the imaginary trigger. My father dies. The lead is cooling off in his heart and brain. And the blood runs from him as it runs from the villain on the screen. His legs quiver for the last time. I see my father trembling as my hands tremble when I sit down to eat at his table. The man is dead now. My father is dead. This is the way I've always wanted to kill him.

From the cinema I walked to the Feddane and sat down on one of the stone benches. Many of them were occupied by visitors from the country, now asleep. There were also men from other cities who were passing through, and people who merely did not want to sleep at home, like me. Boys, youths and old men were sleeping all over the ground and on the benches like fish stranded on a beach. Every little while another arrived and lay down. He would move about for a bit in the spot he had chosen, getting himself comfortable, and then he would be quiet.

I had seventy-five pesetas on me, and I wanted to hide them. But where?

I folded the notes tightly and, taking care to see that no one was watching, buried them in the dirt behind my bench beside a rose-bush.

I slept. My father was chasing me. I felt a hand moving softly in my pocket, but I did not move. My eyes were half-open. It was a man, much older than I. I'll let him look, unless he wants to do more than look. That would be another story. I changed my position so he could go through all my pockets. He stopped searching. I waited for him to start again, but he walked away. I catnapped and had reveries for the rest of the night. One dream finishes in Tetuan and another begins in Tangier. Still in Tetuan, but already in Tangier.

# 7

Already in Tangier, asleep again in a park. I had arrived that evening.

I awoke in a fright. The boy was shaking me by the shoulder and talking to me. Get up! Get up! A raid! The police are coming.

I felt in my back trouser pockets. The sixty pesetas were gone. As we ran, I said: They stole my money.

How much was it?

Sixty pesetas.

We slowed down. You're lucky, he said.

We were both panting. What do you mean, lucky?

They didn't rape you. When there are two or three of them, if they don't find anything on you, they rape you.

What's sixty pesetas? I thought. My arse is worth a lot more than that.

We were in the neighbourhood of the graveyard at Bou Araqia.

Where are we going?

Follow me and don't talk. There's nothing to worry about.

We walked into the world of silence. This was where my little brother Abdelqader had been buried after my father had killed him. When my father dies I'll go to his grave and piss on it. I'll make his tomb into a latrine.

We were walking over the graves, and we stopped in front of a walled-in family mausoleum. The boy leapt over the wall.

Jump. What are you waiting for?

I jumped. In a corner lay a pile of flattened cardboard boxes, and he began to spread them out on the ground.

Here's your place, he told me. Then he made his own spot. I sat down and rested my elbows on my knees. Once he was comfortable, he said: Where are you from?

The Rif.

So you're a Riffian, then?

That's right.

And where are your people?

In Tetuan.

You all live there?

That's right. We used to live here in Tangier, but then we moved to Tetuan.

Did you run away?

Yes.

So did I.

Where are you from?

Djebel Habib.

He's a Djibli, then, I said to myself. Why did you run away?

He began to search in his pockets.

My father's wife threw me out.

And your mother?

She died. He pulled out two cigarette butts. Before offering me one, he said: Do you smoke?

Yes.

He handed me one of the butts. I sniffed at it. Virginia tobacco. He brought out a box of matches and lit it for me. I inhaled a deep breath of smoke, and let it out. A delicious feeling of peace descended upon me.

Do you know Tetuan well? I asked him.

Not very. I ran away and came here after only about two months.

What does your father do?

He's a street porter. And yours?

Nothing. He was in the Spanish army and he deserted. They caught him and gave him two years. He hasn't worked since he got out of jail.

Who works in your family?

My mother. She sells fruit and vegetables in Trancats.

And you? What did you do?

Sometimes I worked for her at the stall and sometimes I had other work.

Why did you run away?

Because my father was always beating me up. Sometimes he'd hang me upside down from the branch of a tree and beat me with his soldier's belt. That was when we lived in Aïn Khabbès.

My father beat me every time his wife told him to.

And what do you do here? I asked him.

I'm a street porter. What else do you expect me to do? After a moment of silence he said: I'm tired. I'm going to sleep.

It was about one in the afternoon when I went down to the port. I felt very weak. At one of the waterfront cafés I asked for a glass of water. Nearby was a stand that sold bean soup. Only one peseta, and I could have a bowl. But where to find the peseta? My life is not worth even one peseta now. After a few minutes of walking in the strong sun I began to feel sharp pains in my stomach. This sun will drive me crazy. I picked up a small fish that lay on the pavement, and smelled it.

The odour was overpowering, unbearable. I peeled off the skin. Then with disgust, with great disgust, I began to chew it. A taste of decay, decay. I chew it and chew it but I can't swallow it. I can't.

From time to time the small sharp stones hurt the soles of my feet. They hurt. I went on chewing the fish as if it were a wad of gum. It was like chewing gum. I spat it out. Its stink was still in my mouth. I looked down with rage at the mass I had spat out. With rage. I ground it into the pavement with my bare feet. I stepped on it. I ground it under my feet. Now I chew on the emptiness in my mouth. I chew and chew. My insides are growling and bubbling. Growling and bubbling. I feel dizzy. Yellow water came up and filled my mouth and nostrils. I breathed deeply, deeply, and my head felt a little clearer. Sweat ran down my face. Running, running. I thought of the boy who had saved me from the police last night. Why didn't he wake me up this morning? Why? Did he try, and couldn't because I was sleeping so heavily? Perhaps he tried. I was sorry we had not given each other our names. I was sorry. The fisherman sat in his boat, eating his loaf of bread. He eats it, and I, I am eating it too as I watch. He leans over the gunwale, and I watch him wearily. I watch and watch, thinking that he may throw something away, something I can eat, as he is eating. The monkey tied to the mast seizes something, and nervously cracks it between its teeth. I hoped the fisherman was chewing without pleasure, the way I had chewed my rotten fish. I watched the loaf of bread avidly. He was gazing distractedly at the waterfront skyline, running his eyes vaguely over old Tangier. Throw away your bread now, the way I threw away my fish, I told him silently. He threw the bread into the water. A delicious taste of salt filled my mouth. Delicious. A feeling of pleasure revived my weak body. In spite of being so tired, I felt better. I stripped off my shirt and trousers, and plunged into the water. I swam beneath the bread and saw that the slab of meat that had been inside it had already sunk to the bottom. There goes half my luck, I thought. The fisherman began to laugh uproariously. I raised my head towards him, my hand clutching the bread. I looked at him and at the bitten piece of bread. Lumps of shit floated all around me in the water. Floating, floating. I squeezed the bread in my hand. It was spongy, and sticky with oil from the boats. That bear is laughing at me as though I were a big fish he was going to catch. He's laughing at me. I've swum into his net. Inside. I began to swim towards the concrete steps, passing other small lumps of shit and bread bobbing in the water in front of my face, bobbing and bobbing. I pushed them away as I swam. In my mind they became connected: bread and shit. Connected. A little water went down my throat, went down. I choked, choked. There was pain in my head and chest. I climbed two of the steps. On the third step I slipped and rolled back down into the water. Again the water ran into my throat. Again. The idea came to me that I was going to go on for ever, climbing up the steps only to slip and fall back into the water. On and on. Even as I got to the highest step, I imagined myself falling backwards into the bay. Falling again. I was very careful where I placed my feet. My body was covered with sticky oil. I picked up my shirt and trousers, and started walking. On my way, I looked behind me and the fisherman waving at me. Laughing. The sound of the laughing dies away little by little. Dies away. Now he has stopped laughing. Stopped.

He called after me, wheedling. Hey, boy! Come here! It's only a joke. Come on. Here's another loaf of bread.

Poor kid, said the fisherman in the boat with him.

I did not turn around and go back towards them. The humiliation was very great. Too great. Ahead of me on the pavement there were some more small fish that had been trampled on. Trampled underfoot. I raised my face to the sky. It was more naked than the earth. More naked. The hot sun struck my face, struck it. I began to tremble with fatigue. I tremble and shake. I see a cat reclining comfortably in a shady corner. It looks at me half-asleep, with indifference. Indifferent. Its white and black belly rises and falls slowly, slowly. I picked up one of the small, dry fish. Dry. It had a worse stench than the first one. Worse than the first. I began to vomit yellow water again. That was what I wanted. I wanted it. I vomited and vomited, until only the sound came out. Only the sound, the tight sound of retching. That was what I wanted. I walked towards the beach, feeling empty, weak. Now and then it seemed that I was about to fall and not get up again. In order not to think about what had happened and what might be going to happen, I began to look back at the footsteps I was making in the sand. The waves broke over them shortly after I made them. I watched my footsteps and the waves. I threw my shirt and trousers down onto the sand and began to rub my body with seaweed and sand. I rub and rub. My hair is even stickier than my body. Stickier. I went on rubbing and rinsing until my skin was red, red. The skin on my body was still sticky with oil, but not so dirty as before.

In the afternoon, after wandering far and wide, I sat down on some steps opposite the railway station. I did not manage to carry any suitcases for the travellers who arrived. I failed. I did not dare approach them. One of the porters yelled into my face: Get back! Out of here! Go on! This was a good town until you all landed here like a swarm of locusts!

They swore at me, spat on me, and shoved me away. A muscular young man gave me a hard kick and chopped me on the back of my neck. But I was determined to stay there. I stayed there. Later I succeeded in persuading a European to let me carry his suitcase. It was heavy. As I was lifting it up to carry it, a big man grabbed me and began to swear at me. He managed to convince the traveller that he was more capable of carrying the bag than I was. Violently he yanked the handle out of my hand. Violently. The situation has not changed at all so far. When I was seven or eight years old I always dreamt about bread. And here I am at sixteen still dreaming about it. Am I going to go on dreaming about bread for ever? The cat on the fishermen's pier was luckier than I. It can eat fish out of the gutter without vomiting. Yes, without vomiting. There's nothing left but begging or stealing. But it seems to me that a beggar sixteen years old is not going to collect much. Yes, it is difficult. Sebtaoui was right: begging is a profession for children and old people. If a young man can't find work, it's more shameful to beg than to steal. That's what he used to say. I wonder where they are now, he and Abdeslam. Who knows?

A young man sat down near me and took out a pack of black cigarettes. Do you smoke? he said. I turned my head and answered weakly: Yes.

76

What's the matter with you? Are you sick?

No.

He came nearer and I took a cigarette from him. He lighted a match.

Thank you. Not now. Thanks.

He got up, saying: Wait for me. I'll be back.

I smelled the cigarette. If I smoke it I'll vomit again without vomiting anything. The same as at noon. I heard the sound of a plane flying overhead, and raised my eyes to the sky. The noise slowly grew fainter, and I did not see the plane. A feeling of sleepiness stole over me. I heard the young man talking. Here!

The cigarette had fallen from my hand. I must have slept. Yes, I've been asleep.

He was holding out half a loaf of bread stuffed with tinned sardines. I saw a bottle of wine in his hand. He took a small glass out of his pocket and filled it. When he had drunk, he refilled it.

Raising the glass to his lips he said: Where are you from?

I answered as I ate. I'm from the Rif. My family lives in Tetuan.

He emptied his glass again and licked his lips contentedly. When did you come to Tangier?

Yesterday.

And where do you sleep?

In the street.

I was happy eating. I swallowed some mouthfuls without being able to chew them. He filled the glass and handed it to me. Do you drink?

Yes, I said, and drank it at one gulp.

I began to feel things getter clearer. I smoked the cigarette and had a second glass. When I had finished the third, he said: Do you want to sleep at my house?

I looked at him surprised. His expression was not reassuring. He wanted something of me, and I thought I knew what it was. Yes, his eyes tell me that's what he wants.

No. Thank you. Thank you very much.

As you like. He shook a few drops of wine out of the glass and put it into his pocket. See you again, he said.

Thank you. Goodbye.

I had almost told him that I slept in the graveyard. Luckily I stopped in time to avoid such stupidity. I walked along the street where the palm trees grew. The soft breeze revived me, and I saw everything clearly in my mind. Then I stopped walking. From a car an old man was signalling to me. What does he want? I went over to the curb and leaned down to the window. He opened the door and said to me in Spanish: Get in.

I got in and sat beside him. He drove slowly. *¿Adónde vamos?* I asked him. He made a circular motion with his hand. A *paseo*, he said. A little *paseo*.

He wants something different, I thought. But I'm not afraid of him. Just what is it he wants, though?

Are you from Tangier? he asked me.

No. I'm from Tetuan.

We were on the outskirts of town. He's a *maricón*. That much is certain, I thought.

He stopped the car in a dark section of the road. The lights of the city sparkled in the distance. He turned on the overhead light. So the short ride ends here. With a caressing movement he runs his hand over my fly. And the other ride begins. Button by button, very slowly, he unfastened the trousers, and my sex felt the warmth of his breath. I did not dare look at his face or even at his hand, whose warm pressure had made my sex rise up.

*¡Bravo!* he was saying. *¡Macho bravo!*

He began to lick it and touch it with his lips, and at the same time he tickled my crotch with his fingers. When he pulled half of it down his throat, I felt his teeth. And if he bites it? I thought. The idea cooled my enthusiasm. To bring it back, I began to imagine that I was deflowering Asiya in Tetuan. When I finished, he still had me in his mouth. He took out his handkerchief and wiped his lips. His face was congested, his eyes very wide, and his mouth stayed open. I buttoned my fly and folded my arms over my chest as if nothing had happened. Taking out a pack of cigarettes, he offered me one and lighted it for me. Then he lit a cigarette and turned on the radio. A beautiful calm music came over the air. I sat enjoying it, and was reminded of Oran and my work with the lovely Monique. Monique! Today it's only a name, to be remembered or forgotten.

We did not say a word to one another as we drove back to the city. He gave me fifty pesetas and let me out near the place where he had called to me. He shook my hand and said: *Hasta la vista*. His hand was warm and smooth. I waved to him. *¡Hasta la vista!*

The air was full of smoke from the car.

They suck it for five minutes and they give you fifty pesetas. Do they all suck, the ones who are like that old man? Are all the *maricones* as nice as he was? Do all the ones who suck have cars, and do they all give fifty pesetas? A new profession, to add to begging and stealing. I must pick one of the three until a further choice appears. One of the three or all of them, depending on the circumstances. And why not? I took out the fifty-peseta note and looked carefully at it. Then I folded it and put it back into my pocket. I was afraid of losing it. If I had been that old man I should have vomited. Does he get the same pleasure from sucking me that I get from sucking a woman's breast? Does he get excited while he does it? My sex still felt warm and sticky between my thighs. Suddenly I was struck by my conscience. What I had done was no different from what any whore does in the brothel. My upright sex was worth fifty pesetas, looked at in that light.

I went into a little restaurant in the Zoco de Fuera and asked for a plate of fried fish and half a loaf of bread. The two men facing me were masons. On the table stood a one-litre Mobiloil can. The three of us took turns drinking tepid water from it. Each time I lifted it I smelled the foul odour it gave off. At the other two tables there were working men, men out of work, and thieves of various kinds. They all ate in silence. There were only the sounds of spoons and dishes and kitchenware, and the voice of the proprietor giving commands to the boy who assisted him. From time to time one of those who has finished eating emits a loud belch, followed by a drawn-out exclamation: *El hamdoul' illah!* I handed four pesetas to the proprietor and went out. It had been hot inside the restaurant. Egyptian and Moroccan music came from the cafés and restaurants. A young drunk, naked to the waist, stood outside the door of one café, cursing Allah in a piercing voice. Two other young men came out of the café, forced him to lean over, and then poured a jar of water over his head. Then they pushed him back into the café. I noticed that they too were staggering. I thought again of the boy who had saved me the night before from the police raid. I wonder if he is asleep in the graveyard now. If I don't find him there shall I sleep there alone?

I went into a *baqal* and bought five Philip Morris cigarettes. I was approaching the entrance of the cemetery, and it occurred to me that a graveyard is the only place you can go into at any hour of the day or night, without having to ask permission. They're right. Why should they have a guard here? There's no money in here. The dead are not afraid. They don't get angry or hit anyone. Each dead man is in his place. When his gravestone crumbles they put another dead one in the same spot.

The cardboard boxes were piled in their place in the corner. Have they caught him? What has happened to him? I spread out some boxes on the ground. Perhaps he will come. I lit a cigarette, took three wax matches and twisted them together to make a torch. Then I held them up to inspect the writing on the marble plaque. I saw from the numbers there that the person had lived for fifty-one years. The numbers were all I could read. He or she, I didn't know which, was no longer living, and I was still here. But what does it mean, a man who was alive and now isn't? What does it mean, that I should be sleeping here in this corner of a family grave? From the tiles and the well-kept plot I can see that the family was a rich one. What does it mean to allow a man sixty or seventy years old to suck on me and then give me fifty pesetas? There must be answers to these questions, but I don't know them yet. The questions come easily, but I am not sure of the answer to any one of them. I thought the meaning of life was in living it. I know the flavour of this cigarette because I'm smoking it, and it is the same with everything. I smoked with great gusto, and then I threw away the cigarette and went to sleep.

I awoke early. A new boy lay asleep in the place of the other one who had saved me. Quickly I felt to see if what remained of the fifty pesetas was still in my pocket. My fortune was there. The boy had been right when he said there was no safer place than the cemetery. I think the human race respects its members more when they are dead than when they are alive.

At Bab el Fahs I bought a pair of rubber-soled *alpargatas* for fifteen pesetas. My feet were dirty. I had breakfast in a café and smoked the first cigarette of the day happily. A new day to live through. What shall I do during this new day? Will I manage to pick somebody's pocket the way Sebtaoui and Abdeslam do in Tetuan? Why not? I must try before what money I have left gives out.

In the middle of the morning I walked into a market. A European woman was buying something at a stall. She paid and put her change purse back into her handbag. Then she caught sight of me, staring fixedly at the handbag. Her eyes seemed to be saying: Aren't you ashamed? And so I felt ashamed, and went out of the market. I spent the whole day letting the alleys swallow me up and spew me out. In the evening I discovered that you could sleep in the Fondaq ech Chijra. You paid only one peseta at the gate in order to get in, and you could sleep where you liked. There are two levels. The animals sleep below and the people above. It was nine o'clock when I went in. A café, a restaurant, small rooms they rented out, shops, fruit and vegetable stands. The Fondaq is like a city. On the stairway I ran into a drunk. He reached out to touch my face, saying: Aha, gazelle! Where are you off to, beautiful? I pushed his hand away violently, ran up two steps and glared at him. He guffawed.

What are you so nervous about? Afraid of me?

In his hand he held an empty bottle. I'm going to fill up this bottle, he said. I'll be back.

He went on downstairs, laughing, and I continued up, feeling more frightened each minute. He called back to me: Wait for me, handsome. I'll be right up. I'm not going·to let you get away.

There were scores of men on the balcony, some of them already asleep, but most of them sitting up, drinking, smoking *kif*, chatting and singing. I caught sight of a drunk hugging a boy. Then he kissed him on the cheeks. One of the others cried: Leave him alone! Not now! Later, later.

No. I'm not going to sleep here, I told myself. I'd rather sleep in the graveyard.

As I started to go back, someone called to me. Hey, beautiful! Come over here with us and make us happy. I did not turn to look. My heart was pounding. I must buy a knife or a razor. I ran down the stairs very fast, stopping only when I got to the animals' quarters. Luckily human beings are not the only thing in the world. I walked over to a dark corner and sat down. Then I smoked a cigarette. Did Allah mean to make the world like this, with such disorder and confusion? The smell of the beasts was very strong. A mare stood beside me. I folded my arms on my knees, bent over, and fell asleep. I slept sitting up because I was afraid of being raped.

All at once I was being drenched with warm, pungent water. I jumped up, terrified. What's that? I cried. The last drops of urine are still trickling from the mare's puckering hole. She takes a step backwards. Quickly I get out of the way, in case she kicks.

At the door the guard asked me if I was coming back.

No! I cried with feeling. I'm not! I'll never come back!

Why? What's the matter? Did they do something to you?

Yes. A mare pissed all over me while I was asleep.

What were you doing sleeping down there? Why didn't

you sleep upstairs on the balcony? Go to a *hammam* and wash before you go to sleep, or you'll be sick.

Keep your advice for yourself, I told him. He slammed the gate after me.

The air was tepid and the streets were empty. Where to go now? To the baths? And my clothes? I am soaked through. I began to scratch.

Three drunks sat singing in front of the entrance to the old Jewish cemetery. As I went past, one of them called to me. Come here! Where are you going?

I looked over my shoulder and kept walking.

Come on, gazelle! He stood up unsteadily and began to follow me. One of the others said: Let him go. Come back here.

The street leading up to the Zoco de Fuera seemed to be the best way out. As I ran I looked back and saw the drunk sitting down again with the others.

I bought a cake of soap in the Zoco Chico. The square was filled with drunks, whores, *maricones* and beggars. In the Calle de la Marina near the Djamaa el Kbira two Moroccan police stopped me.

Your papers, said the first.

I haven't got any papers.

Where do you live?

In Tetuan.

Hearing this, the second one demanded: Where in Tetuan?

In Trancats. Behind the Jewish baths.

Do you know Moulay Ali?

He's a neighbour of ours.

What are you doing here?

Nothing. I came to look for work.

And where are you going now?

I was sleeping in the Fondaq ech Chijra and a mare pissed on me.

A mare!

Yes, a mare. I was asleep downstairs with the animals.

The two men looked at each other, and the second asked

me: Do you know where Dar Debbagh is?

No.

Come with us.

At the corner he pointed out the place, saying: Go in there. You'll find a fountain. Wash yourself, and in the morning wash your clothes.

The water at the fountain was warm. After I had bathed, I washed my trousers and shirt by trampling them underfoot. Now and then from the nearby café there was the sound of men's voices as they argued over their card games. A man staggered out and came over to me.

What are you doing? Are you crazy, washing your clothes at night?

I stopped stamping and explained why I was doing it.

A mare!

Yes. A mare.

Mmmm, he said at length. I see. Well, take a good wash.

When I had finished, there were my wet shirt and trousers on the ground in front of me. There was no other solution. I wrung them out as much as I could, and put them back on.

I stopped walking when I came near to the railway station. Shall I sleep in a freight car or go to the beach? On the sand nobody will ask me any questions, whereas a guard can come through the freight car. The main thing is: will I be able to protect myself against someone bigger than I am?

Again I heard in my head the words of the boy who had taken me to the graveyard: If they don't find anything to steal on you they rape you. I had more than twenty pesetas in my pocket. Will that be enough to protect me? Maybe the boy was right, but he was talking about what they do in the middle of the city. On the beach, or in a freight car, though, they could rob you first and rape you afterwards. They could even cut your throat. And on the beach who could hear? So it's the freight car. I climbed the wall and let myself down. I could feel the sharp points of the gravel through the soles of my *alpargatas*, and I worried that they would cut through. I went along slowly, carefully, until I came to the first freight car. I climbed into it and lit a match. It was empty.

Suppose someone comes along and attacks me, I thought again. I jumped down to the ground and picked out the two sharpest stones I could find. As I climbed back up into the car I heard the soft sound of cloth ripping. My trousers.

Bad luck! I threw myself down on the floor. One stone was in my hand and the other lay beside me, near my head. I must buy a knife. Or at least a razor-blade. And I've got to find a friend somewhere in this city. What has become of the boy who saved me? Is he staying away from the graveyard on purpose? How long will I have to go on living by myself? Ought I to go on accepting this life as it comes up each day, or not?

# 8

We were in the Café Chato, and I had just lost my last centimo playing *aaita*. When we had begun to play, my friend el Kebdani was winning and I was losing. I had had twenty-five pesetas left, and el Kebdani told me: This isn't your lucky day. Stop playing.

Don't worry about me, I told him sharply. I can manage myself and my money.

Now, a little after noon, el Kebdani had just lent me five pesetas. I bought three pesetas' worth of *kif* and paid two for a glass of green tea. We were sitting up on the balcony; through the little window I could see the whole Zoco de Fuera in front of me. It was Sunday. The big square was crowded with circulating salesmen and buyers, as well as the others who were walking through without buying anything. The wind had come up and the sky was dark with clouds. All the Moroccan establishments were shut—restaurants, cafés and shops. Above each doorway there was a Moroccan flag, and tacked beside it a black flag. In some cafés the owners sat playing cards, treating the day as one of leisure. Earlier that morning I had asked Chato what the holiday meant. It's a bad day, he answered in a voice that came half from his mouth and half through his nose.

And what does a bad day mean?

You don't know?

No.

I'll tell you. The thirtieth of March nineteen twelve was the day when the French began to protect Morocco. That was under Moulay Hafid. And today's the thirtieth of March nineteen fifty-two, so it's forty years of protection. And that's why it's a bad day.

But what do we want the French to do today?

Don't you know what we want them to do?

No. What?

We want them to get out! The Protectorate was supposed to last forty years. It expires today.

Do we want the Spanish to get out too?

He looked at me with annoyance. Listen, I haven't got time to talk about it now. Go up onto the balcony and ask one of your friends to tell you all about it.

El Kebdani had won about three hundred pesetas, when he suddenly announced he was quitting.

Finish the game with us, one of the players said angrily.

Suppose I don't feel like it? I have to go on playing anyway?

No, but it's not logical to stop now. You've won everything we had. Finish the game out to the end, since you're the winner.

I'm hungry, el Kebdani said. I'm going to get some lunch.

We're all hungry, they told him. Play cards.

If you don't want to finish the game, divide your winnings.

That's right. Makes sense. That's the thing to do, unless you want to go on with the game.

El Kebdani laughed sarcastically, and took the *sebsi* I had filled for him.

I'm warning you. You'd better finish this game.

It looked as if there were going to be trouble. Chato yelled up: I don't want noise in my café! Go out into the street if you feel like killing each other.

When the gamblers had thinned out, Chato had gone back downstairs. Usually he stayed on the balcony keeping track of the winnings so he could collect his commission. When he had left, I had thought to myself: He wants us out of here. The stakes aren't worthwhile.

Suddenly a furious voice came up from the Zoco de Fuera. People! People! Moroccan patriots! This is a black day. Exactly forty years ago today, in nineteen twelve, the French signed the treaty of the Protectorate over Morocco. And we're still not free.

We all crowded around the window. It's crazy el Merouani, the one who sells the pastries in the Zoco Chico, said el Kebdani.

What's he saying?

What can he say? He's completely out of his head. He's just having some fun with them.

They say he's an informer for the Spanish.

It wouldn't surprise me.

You shouldn't say it unless you're sure. Where'd you hear that?

I know. He belongs to a secret party run by some Spanish who want to get rid of the International Zone so they can run Tangier by themselves.

Again Chato yelled from below:

That's enough up there! I don't want to hear any politics in this café! Go out into the Zoco if you feel like talking politics or fighting.

El Merouani went on shouting in his wild voice, shaking his arms excitedly in the air. Out with colonialism!

Out! Out! shouted the crowd.

Long live free and independent Morocco!

*Aache!* cried the crowd.

Down with the traitors! screamed el Merouani.

*Yasqot!*

Holy war, in the name of Allah!

*El jihad! El jihad ya'ibad Allah!*

A Djibliya woman in a straw hat climbed up onto a wooden crate and began to scream: *Youyouyouyouyouyouyou!*

We ran downstairs and stood looking out over the barrage

of benches and tables that were stacked in front of the entrance.

In his half-mouth, half-nose voice Chato said: Either go outside or back upstairs. Out or up!

I leapt over the barricade and stood outside. Are you coming or not? I called to el Kebdani. He hesitated a moment, and then jumped too.

Come back here! cried one of the players. Don't listen to fuckface there.

The fuckface is your mother, I told him.

He spat at me across the barricade, and I spat back at him. Then he threw a bench out at me. I dodged it, and insulted his mother again.

We'll see about this later, he said. I'll show you who's who. When I get hold of you I'll spit up your ass!

I grabbed my groin and shouted: Come and get it!

Kill each other outside, Chato was saying. Go on out, all of you!

El Kebdani pulled me ahead by the arm. Shit on their mothers, I told him. They want you to stay there. They think maybe they'll be able to get some of their money back.

I was born a long time ago, he said. I know what the sons of bitches want.

They were cheating. Did you notice?

I noticed, yes. But they're idiots. I could follow everything they were doing.

El Merouani was beckoning to the excited crowd, trying to make it go in the direction he wanted. We came nearer to the multitude.

Most of these people are from somewhere else, said el Kebdani. They're not from Tangier.

Where do you think they're from?

The Rif, most of them. Can't you tell by their faces? Look at them! They're Riffians! Aren't they Riffians?

You're right. They certainly look like it. They're from our country.

The crowd had begun to run towards the main bus stop.

Piles of stones lay here and there because the street was being repaved. The men were collecting the stones. Then they went in four principal directions: up the Calle del Estatuto, down the Cuesta de la Playa, through the gate of Bab el Fahs, and into the narrow Semmarine where the money-changers stood. There was another group that ran up to the police station at the top of the steps and began to throw rocks. El Kebdani and I followed the crowd that had gone into the Semmarine. They were stoning a policeman. Some of the stones hit his head. His white helmet fell onto the pavement. The blood ran down his face. He put one hand on the top of his head and the other on the holster of his revolver, and began to run towards the Zoco de Fuera, followed by the stone-throwers. One of them suddenly turned and hurled a rock at a large clock that hung over the entrance to an Indian bazaar. The clock said one fifteen when he smashed it. Then they broke the windows of a shoe store and a camera store beside it.

Let's get some of those watches and cameras, I said.

No.

Why not?

Because we don't know yet what's going to happen. They could stop us and search us.

But look at them all grabbing the watches over there!

Let them grab, if they want. And if they jump into a well, are you going to jump in, too?

There was the crash of more plate glass being broken.

You're crazy, I told him. You're afraid! I didn't think you were like that.

You're the crazy one. Steal by yourself, if you want.

Shots rang out from the region of the police station.

The police have begun shooting, said el Kebdani. Look at what they're doing to the Zapatería Rex!

A group of men came running in our direction, all of them carrying rocks. Women and children were screaming. The peddlers and stall-keepers were abandoning their merchandise and fleeing. El Kebdani pulled my arm. Come on! Run!

We rushed and hid behind the booth of a Jewish moneychanger almost at the entrance of the market. The smashing of the shop windows continued in the Plazuela Pérez Galdós, and the sound of shooting was coming closer. Everyone is running and crying out. The shots are very near. I raised my head and peered out. A man was rolling on the pavement in front of us, blood pouring from him. A Moroccan policeman ran behind, nervously brandishing his revolver.

Duck! cried el Kebdani. Do you want them to kill us?

Look through this crack, I told him. Can you see all right?

Yes. I can see.

I think that one's dead. He's not moving.

I see him. But shut up.

People run and shout. The rapid gunfire comes closer.

A Moroccan youth tried to crawl in with us. We pushed him away. Find another place! Yes, get out of here! There's no room here for you.

Or stay out there where you are until they shoot you, I added.

Three other youths halted in their flight and stood still near us. The two taller ones helped the shorter one climb up onto the roof of a shop. Once he was up there, he looked around quickly and called down: Let's get out of here fast!

The continuous gunfire was louder. A cry, and there is the thump of a body falling to the pavement.

They've got another, I said.

I'm listening and watching, he told me.

A policeman appeared, carrying a machine-gun. As he passed, the short youth uttered a cry, and leapt down on top of him from the roof. We both raised our heads above the booth. The policeman is lying face down, with the young man on top of him, hammering his head with his fist as if he were pounding a nail.

Do you know who that policeman is? said el Kebdani.

No.

That's Inspector Barcia. His father's Moroccan and his mother Spanish.

The youth rose and picked up the machine-gun that lay a

few feet away. Jerkily he turned it this way and that, trying to understand how it worked. But it was no use. He had no idea.

The Inspector lay there unconscious.

Suddenly the young man raised the machine-gun with both hands above his head and, uttering an oath, threw it to the ground with all his might.

*Inaal dinek!*

Then another policeman appeared, firing one shot after another. The short youth spun around, crying out. The policeman fired again, this time hitting him in the belly. He fell and rolled into the gutter.

He got it in the back and front, I said.

I'm watching.

I've never seen a man shot before, I said. Only in the movies.

Well, now you're seeing it before your eyes, said el Kebdani.

They must be killing people like this all over town.

What do you expect them to do?

El Kebdani's forehead was covered with sweat.

Keep calm, I told him.

What are you talking about? he demanded. I don't need your advice.

You're trembling, though, I said.

I'm not trembling, he whispered furiously. Can't you shut up? Do you want them to spill our guts here, like that one out there?

What a coward you are, I murmured.

All right. I'm a coward. But shut up.

A third policeman came into view, shooting one shot into the air. He helped the other one lift the Inspector from the ground where he had been lying. The other picked up the machine-gun and put the Inspector's cap on his head for him. How do you feel? he asked him.

I'm all right. Just dizzy.

I got that dog, the policeman told him.

They walked over to the youth. One of them moved him

with his foot. Then they turned and began to run down the hill towards the Zoco Chico.

Let's get out of here, whispered el Kebdani.

Where to?

Anywhere. If they find us in here we're finished.

There was the sound of more shots approaching.

Come on. Fast, he said.

I climbed out first. Look! The boy's moving. He's still alive!

Hurry! El Kebdani pulled me by the arm. Do you want them to get us too?

We saw the three policemen running down the Siaghines. And we ran down the Calle el Mansour. Halfway down the hill el Kebdani stopped. Wait a minute. I've got to piss.

I felt the need, too. As we stood there leaning against the door of a shop, people came running by. Ahead of us in the Saqqaya we saw a young man lurching along, leaning heavily to the right under the weight of the bag he was carrying. We're in luck, said el Kebdani. Here's Qaabil. We'll go with him up to his shack at Sidi Bouknadel.

El Kebdani had often spoken about Qaabil and how he had worked for him as a *cargador*.

Is that the smuggler you told me about? I said. The one who has so much money?

That's the one. He's got enough to bury you and me from head to foot.

He doesn't look as if he had a hundred pesetas in the world, I told him.

The little square was empty of people. Occasionally a few men ran across it in one direction or another.

Qaabil! cried el Kebdani.

Qaabil stopped walking and set the bag down on the pavement.

Where are you going? el Kebdani asked him.

To the shack. Come on with me. Sallafa's there with Bouchra. I've shaved the dirty bitch's hair and eyebrows.

Qaabil and I carried the bag between us as we climbed the

steps in the direction of Amrah.

What's going on? el Kebdani asked him.

I don't know. When I came out of the *bodega* there was a lot of running around. I didn't see anything more.

Didn't you hear the shots?

I heard a few, but they were a long way off, and I couldn't find out what was happening.

The police are shooting at the Moroccans, said el Kebdani.

What for?

It's the thirtieth of March.

And what are the Moroccans fighting with? asked Qaabil.

Rocks. What do you expect them to fight with?

Are there many dead?

They're shooting at everybody they see, if he's a Moroccan.

A voice from behind us shouted: Clear the way!

A man was carrying a wounded friend on his back, while a third walked behind.

Who's the friend with you? Qaabil asked el Kebdani. What does he do?

He used to sell soup and fish in the street, and he worked at a restaurant in the Zoco de Fuera.


Qaabil's shack was built at the very edge of the high cliffs above the Sidi Bouknadel beach. One of its doors opened onto the cliff. The other gave onto an alley that led downward in the direction of Amrah. It was a real smuggler's shack.

When we went in, Sallafa was groaning a song of Farid el Atrache's: *Forget him who forgets you, and don't regret his loss.* Her hair and eyebrows had been cleanly shaved with a razor, so that now she looked like a handsome boy. She wore a lightweight, black and white striped *zigdoun*. Bouchra was stretched out on the divan in a red and gold brocade caftan with a gauzy *dfin* over it. She had a *sebsi* in her hand. The girls put me in mind of the three days I had spent with Abdeslam and Sebtaoui at Sida Aziza's house, back in Tetuan. I had a thousand pesetas in my pocket at that time, I thought. And today, holes in my pockets and no work.

A *tajine* of fish and potatoes sat on the *taifor*, ready to be served. Sallafa brought us the *tas* with a kettle of water and a cake of soap, so we could wash our hands. She nearly lost her balance while she was pouring the water for el Kebdani. When my turn came she smiled at me. She poured, smiled, and poured again, holding the kettle unsteadily. When she got to Qaabil she began to laugh. He seemed annoyed with her, and pulled the kettle away from her, crying: Let go of that, you dirty whore!

Always talking about your mother, she said.

He made as if to slap her. El Kebdani intervened, taking up the kettle and beginning to pour the water over Qaabil's hands.

The next time I won't just cut off your hair and eyebrows. I'll drop you off the cliff out there.

Try it if you dare, she told him. Just try it, and we'll see who goes over the cliff.

Aren't you two ever going to stop? Bouchra cried.

The *tajine* was excellent, and very heavily spiced. We sat around the table afterwards, until five in the afternoon, mainly talking about the trouble in the streets as we drank our wine, smoked our *kif*, and listened to old records by Om Kaltoum.

I had already fallen asleep on the divan, when el Kebdani called out my name sharply. Mohamed! We're going out. Stay here with the two girls until we get back. Go back to sleep if you like.

All right. I'll sleep a little.

I heard them shut the door and turn the key in the lock. Sallafa and Bouchra both lay asleep, Bouchra on her right side facing the wall. Sallafa lay on her stomach, with her face also towards the wall. She lay like someone who had been dragged out of the sea. It seemed to me that her buttocks needed to be given first-aid treatment. As I was dropping off to sleep, I heard her move. Then she said: Has that dog gone out?

Slowly I opened my eyes. She had got up and was turning on the light. So you weren't asleep after all, I thought.

She stretched in such a way that she managed to project her

bosom and her buttocks at the same time. Then she stood up straight and looked at me archly. Her eyes seemed half-asleep.

Are you asleep too? she asked me.

I pulled myself up into a sitting position. I'm just resting a little, I said.

She lifted the half-empty bottle of wine and indicated the two glasses on the table. Come into the other room so we won't wake up Bouchra.

Shall I go in or not? I said to myself. Why not? She's the boss here, the mistress of the house.

When I got to my feet I realized that my head was heavy. There was a dull pain in my right temple. I glanced at Bouchra, wondering if she too were awake. She's attractive, but I don't dare go near her.

What difference does it make? I thought. I'll follow Sallafa into the other room. Women have their own system. They know how to act in such cases.

I walked into the room. It was a completely furnished bedroom, not at all what I had expected to see in a shack. In one corner there was a high pile of cartons. Perhaps they contained some of Qaabil's contraband. She was sitting on the edge of the bed. I sat down on a couch facing her.

Sit over here by me, she told me.

I hesitated.

Are you afraid of Qaabil?

It's not that, I finally said. I just met him. El Kebdani and I were in the street when they were shooting. We were on our way down from the Zoco de Fuera to the Saqqaya.

Even if he finds you here with me, he won't do anything. I know him. A dog that barks.

He might not do anything, I was thinking, looking at her. He might just throw me out of the shack and go on living with you, if he loves you. And there's no doubt he loves you. From what I've seen and heard, it's you who manages him, and that means he loves you.

I rose and went to sit beside her on the bed. She filled the two glasses herself. Then she reached out to the table beside the bed and lit a cigarette. Her eyelashes were black and her eyes were bloodshot. She placed the cigarette between my lips and lit a second one. I thought of Lalla Harouda back at the brothel in Tetuan, and of how she had done the same thing. Today everything is different. Today is better than yesterday.

And if Bouchra should wake up? I said.

She's my sister.

Your sister!

Well, like my sister.

Ah! I see.

She smiled as she looked at me. Her lips are tiny, like a ring for the finger. I had heard that a small mouth on a girl indicated a very tight sex. I smiled back at her. She finished her drink. I was thinking of the boy who had been shot by the police. She took my hand and lay back, looking up at the ceiling as she smoked. From time to time she squeezed my hand. She too must be thinking of something. Her hand is warm. Her long slim fingers seem made to nibble on. I lay down beside her and smoked, staring up at a doll that hung on the wall. I press her fragile hand, thinking of the boy who had come and tried in vain to get behind the booth with us. I felt sorry now that we had not let him in.

The short young man sprang, landing on top of the policeman. He pounds his head as if he were driving in a nail. The second policeman comes, and he is rolling on the pavement.

We stayed a while quietly, she with her hand in mine. I wondered if Qaabil enjoyed tranquil moments like this with her. She stirred. So did I. We looked at each other and smiled.

Wait, she said. I'll undress. She snuffed out her cigarette in the ashtray. Ideas of ecstasy tickled the inside of my head as she pulled off her clothing. Her panties are pink and she wears no brassiere. Her breasts are tiny, like two lemons. My mind went back to the time when I had sucked the oranges on the tree woman at Oran.

Get undressed.

It's better if I keep my clothes on. If Qaabil and el Kebdani should come back I wouldn't have time to get dressed.

They won't be back for another three or four hours, she said.

Where do you think they went?

I don't know. He never tells me where he's going. But whenever he goes out he stays a long time, especially if he has one of his friends with him, because then he feels more daring and does crazier things. Maybe they've gone to the whorehouse together. That's what I think, if you want to know.

Her face was heart-shaped, white, with pink cheeks. It was also the face of a boy. I shut my eyes and let my head fall onto her warm breast. A pillow of flesh, I said to myself. I've got my head on a pillow that's pulsing with life. All I could think of was the cushion under my head, and how beautifully it calmed the pain in my temple. She buried her fingers deep in my hair, and I reached out blindly for her head, forgetting that it had been shaved. The hard short hairs tickled my palm. When I rubbed them the wrong way they stood up. Why did he shave off her hair and eyebrows? He must have been jealous. I licked the hard nipples. Then with delight I began to suck on her right breast, filling my mouth with it. I could feel the tight hard part in the middle of the softness. When I tried to do the same with her left breast, she laughed, squirmed, and covered it with her hand. She tries to direct me back to the right breast, and I keep insisting on the left one. The left breast must be very sensitive. It becomes a game, and soon she cannot bear to have either breast touched. We go on for a little while with the game, both of us laughing.

I'm ticklish on that side.

You're ticklish on both sides now.

She laughed and pulled off her panties. Then with a smile she unbuttoned my fly. The blind dragon rose up and stood rigid in her hand. She smoothed it briefly from its head to its roots, and set to work rubbing it against the lip between her legs. The hairs of the black triangle there are as rough as those on her scalp. The dragon feels the roughness as he scrapes his bald head on them.

I want to go inside, but she wants only to rub. She squeezes it, chokes it, measuring its size at one end and the other with her hand. I pulled away from her. Then she let me inside and hugged me with her arms and legs. I imagined talking to my sex: There you are, dragon! Blind and bald. This is your first combat in Tangier. Fix it so she'll never forget you. Be strong whether you like it or not.

It was Bouchra's voice that awoke me. Get up, Sallafa! Are you asleep?

I sat up quickly. Has el Kebdani come back? I asked her. Not yet.

I went out into the larger room. From there I heard Sallafa saying to Bouchra: Hasn't the pimp got here yet?

I'm afraid they may have arrested them and taken them to the police station, with all the trouble in the street.

They can take them all the way to Hell, Sallafa said.

I went into the latrine. My sex was limp and stuck to my thighs. I came out and sat down with Bouchra. She seemed preoccupied, even sad. I watched her. Something was bothering her. Sallafa bustled in, she looked at me, smiled, and came over to me, leaning above me. Then she took my face in her two hands, and stroked it. Finally she gave me a resounding kiss on the lips, the way one kisses a baby. I smiled.

She went into the latrine and shut the door. I remembered the day in Aïn Ketiout when the girl gave me brown bread with butter and honey and put perfume on me and kissed my lips, and I told her I was leaving with my family for Tetuan. Where can she be now? It's a different situation here with Sallafa. I looked at Bouchra, sitting dejectedly with her elbows on her knees and her head between her hands. The way she sat reminded me of the way my mother had sat after she had heard that they had caught my father. Presently she got up, went to the phonograph and put on a record. *Oukkeddibou Nafsi* it was, with Om Kaltoum singing. It made me think of Aïn Khabbès in Tetuan and the hashish-smokers and drunks at the café where I had worked.

The key turned in the door and I sat up. El Kebdani came in first, then Qaabil. They looked tired.

What news? I asked el Kebdani.

He turned down the volume on the phonograph.

It's all over, he said. A lot of Moroccans are dead or wounded.

Qaabil went into the bedroom. El Kebdani sat down facing me. Sallafa came out of the latrine.

Where have you been? she asked el Kebdani.

We had something to do.

Why don't you admit you went to a whorehouse? she said, laughing. You went to Seoudiya el Kahala's. Or else it was Zohra el Hamqat's.

Before el Kebdani could answer, Qaabil shouted: Are you going to shut that dirty mouth?

Whose dirty mouth? Yours?

She went into the bedroom. El Kebdani got to his feet.

Let's go out for a little while, he said. We can come back later.

We went out through the other door that gave onto the cliffs and the beach below. The cold wind slapped my face. We lit cigarettes and stood there. The lights of the ships anchored in the harbour were brilliant.

I've got something important to tell you, said el Kebdani.

What is it?

Qaabil has agreed to let you work with us tomorrow.

Yes. That is important, I said.

But on one condition. You have to stay up here at the shack tonight and all day tomorrow. At least, until the time comes to go to work.

I was thinking: That's just what I want. It's a condition that's fine with me.

To him I said: But why?

I'll tell you why. Qaabil doesn't know you yet, and he's afraid you might talk to somebody.

And you? You think—

He interrupted me. No! But then, I know you. I told him about you, and that persuaded him. I said you were serious and honest and tough.

Good, I said.

You see, he's had a lot of trouble with his *cargadores*. He's sure the only reason he had this run-in with the Customs and the secret police was that he used new *cargadores*. Half the time it's the police themselves who send out the *cargadores* to work with the smugglers. That way they find out where the work's going to be done, what time it's going to happen, and even what's going to be moved in. The police give them three or four times as much as the smugglers do.

I didn't know that, I said.

They feel protected, you see. After a pause he went on: Qaabil's a good man. The only trouble with him is that he's stingy. If you want to get what's coming to you, you practically have to steal it from him.

I laughed.

He's only generous with women. With girls like Sallafa, for instance.

We both laughed. Is he jealous of her? I asked him.

He knows she'll open her legs to anything. Even a monkey.

And in spite of that he loves her?

That's right.

But why did he shave off her hair?

He's crazy about her. He cut off her hair and eyebrows so she wouldn't go very far from the shack. Sometimes she'll wander off and stay ten days or more, and he's like a maniac the whole time.

Where does she go when she runs away like that?

She gets drunk and stays with friends. Where would she go?

Do you think she loves him?

He laughed. Yes, she loves him, he said with irony. Does a woman like that love anybody? All she wants is the cash. I've heard her say it straight out. One day I heard her tell him: You're wasting your time with me. Look for another one to love, she said. Get it into your head that I don't love you!

And what does he say when she talks to him like that?

What do you expect him to say? Either he doesn't answer, or he threatens to beat her up. But I've never seen him lift a finger to her.

I've noticed. But in spite of all she says, he still loves her. He's a strange one.

He thinks she's worked magic on him.

And you? Do you think she's got him under a spell?

I don't believe in spells, he said. He loves her, and that's all there is to it.

But how did he ever manage to cut off her hair?

He got her drunk, and then he put hashish in her tea. When she passed out he got to work on her with the razor.

And when she woke up?

She smashed a few dishes and swore she'd get even with him. But she's like him. She won't do anything.

And Bouchra?

Bouchra's her best friend. Sallafa goes crazy when she's separated from her.

Hasn't Bouchra got a lover?

I don't know, he said slowly. I think the only one she likes is herself. She's hard to get on with. But she's a nice girl. Not a mean bone in her body. She only talks when she has to.

I saw that.

We lighted more cigarettes. I thought of telling him what had happened between me and Sallafa, but I was afraid he might turn out to be jealous, or might envy me for my good fortune. Or he might go out of loyalty to Qaabil and tell him.

When we went back into the shack the penetrating voice of Om Kaltoum was singing:

*I'm jealous of the lucky glass that touches your lips.*
*And I would stop it from reaching them.*

# 9

All morning Sallafa and I stayed at the shack. Qaabil and el Kebdani had gone without giving me any idea of their plans. Bouchra had decided to visit her mother, whom she had not seen in several days. I assumed that Qaabil and el Kebdani had gone to arrange for the passage of the contraband that we would be moving later.

Sallafa was cleaning the bedroom. I reclined in the *sala* smoking, uneasy in my mind. I called out to her: Have you got a glass of wine in there?

She loomed in the doorway. Wait a minute. We'll open a bottle and drink it together. She smiled and disappeared.

We've really begun a game of love, I said to myself. The present situation here in the shack made me think of the morning long ago when the owner of the pear tree in Aïn Ketiout had shut me into his storeroom. But I also saw differences. At least I am free now to decide whether to stay or leave, even though leaving would mean breaking down the door.

I rose and stood on the divan, leaning out of the window and looking down at the sea below. The sky was cloudy and the water was rough. A few ships, both large and small, were going by. She came up and stood behind me, putting her hands on my shoulders.

What are you looking at? she murmured. I could feel the heat of her breath in my ear. Have I become her lover? Poverty and love go together. What a world!

I'm looking at the ocean. I've never been on a ship in my life, have you?

Who, me? Ask me instead if I've ever been outside Tangier. I've never been anywhere at all, either by land or water.

You've never been out of Tangier?

Never! Why would I? Where would I go? Who would I go with? I've got a feeling that if I should leave Tangier I'd never come back. Never! No, I'd never come back.

Why not?

I don't know.

I turned to face her, and her eyes opened very wide, as if she were going to say: Isn't that the right answer?

I could not go on looking at her, and I let my gaze drop. This girl was beginning to worry me. I looked at the door instead. Then she too turned towards the door, and said again: What are you looking at?

I'm looking at the door.

Why? What's wrong with it?

Nothing.

What are you thinking about? You're thinking of something.

I'm thinking of the door, I said.

What's the matter with the door?

I don't like to be locked in.

We sat down. She had put two glasses and a bottle of wine on the *taifor*.

It used to bother me to have somebody turn the key on me, but I've got used to it. She smiled.

I'm not used to it, I said. And I don't want to get used to it, either. I might as well be in jail.

I was thinking that in the face of that locked door we were equally powerless, she and I. She's Qaabil's girl. And I'm his *cargador*, but one he still doesn't trust. The idea came to me to go over and break down the door, but that would ruin everything: my friendship with el Kebdani, my affair with Sallafa, and the possibility of working for Qaabil and perhaps becoming as trusted a *cargador* as el Kebdani.

What are you thinking about? That's enough thinking! Open the bottle.

I picked up the corkscrew.

I've got something to say to you, she went on.

I looked at her. What's that?

Why don't we leave Tangier? Run away together?

I looked harder at her. Where to?

Anywhere. Casablanca, for instance.

I thought of saying: What about your hair and eyebrows? But I was afraid of hurting her, so I said: And what would we do there?

Anything. All sorts of things.

I opened the bottle.

I'm not a skilled worker in anything, I said. And what would you do in a place like Casablanca?

I can do any kind of work, she declared.

I filled both glasses.

I could work as a maid with a French family, for instance. I have a friend named Fadila. She went to Casablanca. And in no time at all she found a job with a French family.

At this point I remembered what el Kebdani had told me the night before about how Sallafa became whenever she was separated from Bouchra. What about Bouchra? I asked her.

Oh, she'll go with us too.

Is this girl out of her mind? I thought.

I see, I said brusquely.

She's all right, objected Sallafa. What's the matter with her? Don't you think she's all right?

I stared at her.

I didn't say anything against her. I just asked you.

You don't know her yet, she told me. When you get to know her, she'll be just like your sister.

The way she is for you, I said to myself. I passed one of the glasses to her. She took it, and then held it out to my lips for me to drink from. At the same time, she directed the glass I held in my hands to her own lips. We drank slowly, our arms hooked. If I had broken down the door and gone out, I should not have had the pleasure of this moment. Never before had I drunk in this fashion with anyone. The expression in her half-closed eyes, plus a slight movement which she made towards me, said clearly that she wanted my lips. She began to give me, little by little, all the wine that was in her mouth. That also was something I had not experienced before. I am discovering all kinds of new things. This time it was I who led her into the bedroom.

We were already back in the *sala* when I heard the key turn in the lock. Farid el Atrache was singing: *When will you return, love of my soul?* Sallafa had been sitting pensively, listening, neither happy nor sad. I understand her only when she is laughing or quarrelling. It had been good in bed, better than yesterday, or so it seemed to me. Who knows what's passing through her head at this minute? Perhaps she's annoyed because I gave her no precise answer when she made her suggestion that we run away together to Casablanca. I watched el Kebdani come in, carrying a basket of food from the market. He seemed tired and depressed.

Ah, Qaabil! You're back? I cried. He stared at me, and I began to stammer apologies.

I'm sorry. I was thinking of something else. What's the news?

The news is bad. Terrible!

What? *Kheir, insha'Allah!*

He set the basket down in front of Sallafa.

Here. Qaabil says to fry all the fish.

She glared at him. Is this a time to be bringing back food for lunch? she demanded.

We were busy setting up a job.

I don't care what you were busy doing. One of you could have brought the stuff back long ago.

Has something happened, or what? I asked el Kebdani.

It's all clear now, he said. It was the Spaniards who

engineered the riots. They hired the mob and brought it in from outside.

Ah, so what they said about el Merouani at the Café Chato was true, then.

Maybe. Who knows? All we know is that the Spanish started it.

I see! They used the anniversary as an excuse to start things, and then they used the Moroccans as pawns.

It looks that way.

That's very bad.

We know dozens of people were killed, and yet only six or seven funeral processions have gone through the Zoco Chico on the way to the mosque.

And all the other bodies?

They must be hiding them so the public won't see how many there are. Most of the ones who were killed are from out of town. That's why it's so easy for them to bury them in secret.

I thought for a moment. Then I said: Are they letting people walk freely around the city?

Yes, but there are guards everywhere. It'll probably go on like this for several days. The soldiers are working hand-in-hand with the police. They search anybody they think looks suspicious, and take whoever they want to headquarters for a grilling.

Where's Qaabil?

He went to his father's house. Hasn't Bouchra come back yet?

Not yet, Sallafa said. Why don't you go and get her? She may be afraid to come back alone, with all the police and soldiers in the street. Go on, Kebdani, she coaxed.

I don't know where her mother lives, he said.

In Dar el Baroud, near the Café Makina.

But I don't know the house.

Ask anybody down there. There are always children playing in the street. They all know her.

Wait a while. She'll be along. I tell you there's nobody in

the street to ask. In times like this nobody goes out unless he has to. And as for children playing in the street, I didn't catch sight of one anywhere all morning.

*Khlass!* she cried. Come on! Life has suddenly changed? It's the end of the world? Just say you don't want to go. That would be enough.

That's not true, he began.

Don't try to talk!

After a moment she went on, but as if speaking to herself: I know what I'm going to do. I swear, if you find me still around here you can spit on me. You can piss on me!

Everything's all set, he told me. Expect to work tonight. There'll be three other *cargadores* going with us, and we'll be using two cars, one to hold the stuff and the other for the men. I'll be bringing the stuff in from the ship in a rowboat. You'll be on the shore with the other three, and you'll carry it up from the beach to the car. You'll need all your strength, because you've got to move fast the whole time. And you'll need your nerve. The Customs men may be there on the shore somewhere, or stop us at the edge of town. If that happens, you're to do whatever either Qaabil or his partner tells you. You'll meet his partner. The secret police could come up while you're emptying the stuff out of the car, once you get to town. I like to tell you right out. The job is dangerous. It's a job where anything can happen. They may shoot at us. You understand that?

Yes. I understand.

Sometimes the leader is able to bribe them. But usually they can't get together on the amount, and that's when the trouble begins. That's the point when things begin to get rough.

How rough?

I mean they shoot it out.

So Qaabil has a pistol, I thought. That's something to know. I must be very careful with Sallafa. What was there to stop him from firing on us both if he found us in bed together?

110

Has Qaabil got a gun? I asked him.

Ah! That's none of your business. I'm just telling you what may happen. It doesn't matter one way or the other to you and me whether Qaabil and his partner have guns or not. You understand?

I was just asking.

I tell you things I couldn't tell any other *cargador*, he said.

I know. And thanks.

He turned and called out: Where's the *sebsi*, Sallafa?

She was in the kitchen. I don't know, she shouted. Look for it.

She's getting even with him, I thought. I suddenly remembered that we had smoked a little *kif* while we had been in the bedroom; nevertheless I pretended to look for the pipe along with him there in the *sala*. Then he went into the bedroom and called out: Here it is! I've found it!

I went and put on a record. It was Mohamed Abd el Wahab singing 'When Afternoon Comes'.

# 10

I got into the car with the three other young *cargadores* and the old man who was driving. I was the youngest. In spite of the strong smell of wine that came from the driver, he drove carefully. The speedometer never showed more than seventy kilometres an hour, and on curves and inclines it dropped to forty or thirty. We got to Cape Spartel about two in the morning, and drew up behind a large black sedan that stood there.

The door of the other car opened, and a tall, powerful-looking man got out. I guessed that he was about forty-five years old. He came casually over to our car.

How's the road? he asked the driver.

Fine. We didn't see anybody.

We all got out, with the exception of the driver. From their conversation I understood that they were referring to the police and Customs men. And I realized that this tall man was Qaabil's partner.

Now's the time to be men, he told us. Then he put his hand on my shoulder and looked intently at me. What part of the Rif are you from? he said.

Beni Chiker. My name is Choukri.

I know the Chikriyine. The Riffians are tough.

He removed his hand. I know the Riffians, he said again.

I was with them in the Civil War in Spain. I hope you're a real Riffian like the others.

I smiled.

He pulled out a pack of cigarettes and held it out to each of us in turn. It's a good beginning, I thought. He looks like a good man to deal with. Compared to him, Qaabil seems like a boy. He too may be a good man, but you sense his weakness. Whereas it would be easy to feel loyalty to this man.

Are you ready? he asked us, and we all said: Yes.

The path downward was hard to negotiate. We squeezed between trees, crashed through bushes, and clambered over boulders. Are we going to try to carry the stuff back up this same path? I wondered.

Call me Kandoussi if you want to call me anything, said Qaabil's partner.

I decided that this was probably not his real name. It might be only his business name. The path went on being difficult. Several times I stumbled into holes and scraped myself on the sharp rocks.

You've got to be very careful not to fall once you've got the stuff on your back, he said. What we're carrying is fragile.

What could be in the cartons? I thought. Something breakable. What could that be?

When we reached the strip of beach at the bottom of the cliffs he pulled a flashlight out of his pocket and began to make signals with it in the direction of the water. The signals came back from the darkness out there.

We found Qaabil sitting alone on the sand. Beside him lay a pile of sacks and a coil of rope. Ah, you got here! he cried. Everything ready?

Everything's perfect so far, replied Kandoussi.

Soon we heard the sound of a motor. More messages flashed from the water. Kandoussi sent back the same succession of flashes. The sea was rough. The motor came nearer.

Get ready, said Kandoussi.

The sound of the motor stopped.

After a quarter of an hour of silence, there were more signals, which Kandoussi answered.

The rowboat's on the way, he said. Get down to the edge of the water.

Two of the *cargadores* took off their trousers and sandals. The rowboat hove into view, rising and falling with the movement of the waves. The two *cargadores* waded into the water and guided the craft inward, one on each side of it. Kandoussi ran down to the water, and they pulled the boat up onto the beach. There were nine cartons. We began to carry them to a spot not far from the edge of the water, where we stacked them on the sand. The cartons were not as big and heavy as I had expected. Whatever was in them must be very valuable. Watches, perhaps? Rapidly we emptied the boat.

Can you get back to the ship all right? Kandoussi was saying to el Kebdani. It's not too rough?

It's all right.

If you think there's any danger, we'll leave the boat beached here until the morning and take it back then.

No. I don't think I'll have any trouble.

Look out for those rocks.

I know, said el Kebdani. I know the whole place.

See you soon, I said to him.

Ah, Mohamed? *B'slemah.* I'll see you back at the shack in an hour.

The two *cargadores* began to pull the rowboat back out into the water, with el Kebdani plying the oars. I watched him disappear into the darkness, riding up and down on the waves.

Working quickly, we put two cartons into each sack. When we had tied up the openings, Kandoussi came up to me and said: Can you carry two cartons, or is one enough for you?

I can carry three if you want, I said with great confidence.

Probably he doesn't believe me. My body is very thin. But I had my pride. I was thinking: This is better than begging or stealing. And better too than letting an old man suck on me, or selling *harira* and fried fish to the Djebala in the Zoco de

Fuera. Better than any of the work I've had. It's an adventure, and I feel like a man. In any case, I am seventeen. I feel on this early morning that I am entering into a new phase of my life.

We loaded the sacks on our backs, and started up the same path we had come down. Kandoussi went first, and Qaabil, empty-handed, brought up the rear. Each one of us *cargadores* was carrying a sack with two cartons in it. Kandoussi carried the ninth carton, also wrapped in its sack.

It was not long before my load began to weigh more and more heavily on me. The pain hit my spine and the nape of my neck. I must have placed the sack in the wrong position when I took it onto my back. But now I did not dare stop and shift it for fear that Kandoussi would think I was tired, and we were still only about halfway up the path. If I show signs of weakness now, very likely he will not hire me the next time he needs a *cargador*. As for Qaabil, at the moment he seems as unnecessary to the scene as he is ineffective in his daily life. Should I even obey his orders if he gives them? Then I wondered why I should be thinking such things about him. Up to now he has treated me very well. I must try and get rid of these feelings. I must fight against them, even while my shoulders shoot pains in every direction and the bones at the back of my neck go on cracking. I was breathing heavily through my mouth, and my throat was getting dry. I suppose the trouble came from having smoked too much Virginia tobacco and *kif*. But Sallafa also had a part in my weakness. During the past day I had made love with her four times. And here I was, thinking of doing it again. Yes, I'm going to make love with her. There's no doubt about that, if only everything goes well here and I manage to get to the shack before Qaabil and el Kebdani. But the key? Will Qaabil give it to me when we've finished here, if for instance he finds that for some reason he has to stay on longer than he thought, or if he can't get back until morning? The idea of getting into bed with Sallafa at this hour of the morning excites me, and that helps me forget the pain of the load on my shoulders and the

116

burning shortness of breath. The money I was going to get for this work meant nothing compared with what I should find in the shack. Money was only for the world outside the shack. I wish Sallafa were with us now, just walking ahead of us without carrying anything. Am I myself beginning to fall in love with her? Merely to think of her makes my heart beat harder. Then I feel a wave of hostility towards her. I imagine myself insulting her, slapping her, trying to work up her temper. Maybe I like her better angry than calm, better sad than happy. Maybe she means more to me when she is being crazy than when she is sensible. I like the way she behaves when she is with Qaabil. Yes, I like to watch her fight with him. I can imagine myself in Qaabil's place when she disappears, losing control like him and waiting desperately for her return. Thus at this point I learn a new truth about my feelings for Sallafa.

When we got up to the road, the two drivers were there, one standing beside each car. They helped us pile the boxes into the back seat of the first car. Kandoussi got into the front of that car and Qaabil got in with us. We went ahead of Kandoussi, whose car followed always at the same distance, about a hundred metres behind. We drove so slowly that I decided this must have been arranged beforehand, perhaps as a way of protecting the merchandise. I doubt that any of the *cargadores* knew exactly where we were going. During the entire ride no one spoke a word. From time to time the *cargador* sitting to the right of me coughed and sniffed violently. We took the road past the animal cemetery by the river at Boubana. When we got to the crossroads by the Spanish Cemetery both cars stopped, and Qaabil got out. The driver of the other car came over.

Qaabil spoke to our driver. Take them wherever they want to go.

He handed me the key. Go to the shack, and don't open up for anybody but el Kebdani.

The other driver got in and sat in Qaabil's seat. Then we drove down the road towards Dradeb, leaving the other car still parked. The operation had certainly been very carefully planned. I was sure now that Kandoussi and Qaabil trusted absolutely no one. After our car is gone they're going somewhere that only the two of them know about, to unload the stuff. Qaabil must have another key, otherwise he would have said something about my letting him in. He may work all night and not come back before morning.

We got to the hill at Dradeb. The driver smelled even more strongly of wine now than he had before. Where do you want to go, brothers? he asked.

Two of the *cargadores* wanted to be left in the Zoco de Fuera. I asked him to take me to the Place de la Casbah.

I know where to take you, he told me.

The one who had been coughing beside me also wanted to go to the Casbah. I looked at him, and he looked at me, but we said nothing.

The two *cargadores* got down in the Zoco de Fuera, as two policemen walked past. The car drove on through the arch of Bab el Fahs. The streets were empty. Another pair of policemen stood in front of an apartment house. My fear was that they might stop us and ask to see our papers. It was then that I realized how much colder the night was now than it had been earlier. We got out of the car in the Place de la Casbah, the last *cargador* and I, leaving the two drivers together.

I'm going down here towards Amrah, I said to the *cargador*. And you?

He coughed. I'm going down that way, too, to Oued el Ahardan. We passed under the arch and started down the hill. I did not dare bring up the subject of the work we had just done. After a silence he said: Is el Kebdani a friend of yours?

Yes.

He's a good man. This is the first time you've worked like this?

Yes, it's the first time.

And Qaabil, is he a friend of yours, too?

No, he's a friend of el Kebdani's. I met Qaabil through him. Are you a friend of Qaabil's?

No, I only know Kandoussi. He's a man with a lot of guts. And he's serious. He knows what he's doing. If he tells you he's going to do something, he does it. All the *cargadores* want to work for him.

I feel the same way, I told him. I noticed how he treated us.

When we got part of the way down the hill, I stood still and pointed up the small street that led off to the left. I'm going up here to Qaabil's shack, I said.

Yes, he said. So you live with Qaabil?

No. He just invited me to stay there. I haven't got my own place to sleep yet. El Kebdani introduced me to him. I told you.

I know. See you.

*B'slemah!*

I heard only my own footsteps in the dark, silent street. Then there was a shrill scream from two cats nearby. One of them ran in front of me, the other pursuing it. He's after her, I thought. But she wants to get away from him. I hoped Sallafa would not refuse me the delight of being with her at this early hour. To make love early in the morning before dawn! This will be the first time I shall have gone to bed with a woman at the hour of the *fjer*. A first experience.

I got to the shack, and stuck my ear to the door. Once again I heard the yelling of the cats, but from a distance. I slid the key carefully into the lock and opened the door.

There was a light in the bedroom. Is she still awake? I shut the door and turned the key, locking it. Then I gave the key an extra half-turn so that the door could not be unlocked from the outside. I tiptoed into the bedroom. A half bottle of wine sat on the *taifor*, and beside it the *sebsi* and the box of *kif*. She is lying on her right side with her knees drawn up. It's sad to see a girl sleeping alone.

I went back into the *sala* and turned on the light. Two blankets and two pillows had been tossed onto the couch. Now I understood. A pillow and a blanket for me, and the same thing for el Kebdani. I took off my jacket and trousers, remaining in my underwear. There was a sound from the bedroom. When I went in to look, she had changed her position. She was still lying with her knees bent, but now she was facing in the other direction. I sat down on the edge of the bed and put my hand on her shoulder, hesitant to awaken her. It would be better to get into the bed behind her, and then run my hands over her until she wakes up and feels me there beside her. I climbed slowly into the bed.

Then she said very clearly: Your feet are like ice. Get them away from me.

What's the matter? Are you angry with me?

She did not reply. My right hand began to touch her body here and there. It's like an orchard, I thought. There are apples and oranges up here, and pears and peaches back here. And here between her thighs are persimmons. When my hand arrived there, she pushed it away with force.

Don't touch me, she said. It's the wrong time of the month. Go to sleep.

You mean you've got blood? I said incredulously.

Yes. Of course I have. What do you think?

I remembered Monique in her bathroom, sitting on the bidet, washing the blood from between her legs. So now Sallafa is the way Monique was.

I understand, I said. How long does it last?

Oh, at least three days.

So the hope of making love early in the morning is gone, I thought. I may have the chance again some time, and I may not. Who knows what will happen between us in the next few days? My sex is standing alone in the region of the peaches. When it tried to walk a little back and forth, she moved suddenly and lay on her back, saying: Haven't you any shame at all? That's something I won't do with you.

Just a little walk, that's all.

What are you talking about? she cried. Are you crazy, or what?

I'm going to follow this through to the end, I said to myself.

Why not? I asked her.

Because that's something you don't do with women. It's a sin. Don't you know that?

A sin?

Of course. A sin.

I lay on my back now, as she was doing, and looked at the place where the blanket pointed upward, where my sex stood alone. The pressure of the blanket hurt a little, and I arranged it so it would lie back on my belly. How to make it rest? It's stubborn. This was the first time I had been made aware of how extremely stubborn it was. I took hold of her hand and held it for a moment. Then I brought the hand up and placed it on my sex. She said nothing. At the touch of her hand, the sex grew even more eager. I waited for her to play with it as she had done the first night. But her hand merely remained holding it tightly. When I placed my hand over hers and pushed it back and forth, she pulled away from me.

Leave me alone. Can't you just go to sleep? Her voice was plaintive.

This time it was my own hand instead of hers that moved back and forth. I started to give it a workout and a rubdown.

What are you doing?

Without looking at her I said: Just let me alone. I've got to satisfy it or it won't ever lie down.

You're going to get me filthy, she said. Go into the other room and do whatever it is you want to do.

I got out of bed, imagining that I was about to seize Asiya by the tank, and walked into the other room holding my sex in my hand so it would not get cold. But I had to use both hands to cover myself with the two blankets. I quickly gave it back the warmth of my hand, so it would not weaken.

About nine o'clock in the morning we had breakfast together in the *sala*. We did not speak. She looked pale, sad and dreamy. I too felt tired and depressed as a result of the imaginary rape. Is it not a kind of insanity to conjure up the image of a woman and then proceed to rape her? And I do not even know whether the girl is still living. It would have been better to have stayed there in bed, warmed by Sallafa's body, feeling her alive and moving beside me. I could have touched her and smelled her. Asiya was only a great void in my imagination, and I had worked myself into a frenzy of excitement over this nothingness.

Neither el Kebdani nor Qaabil arrived. Could something have happened to el Kebdani? It was normal enough for Qaabil not to have appeared, but I was worried that el Kebdani might have fallen into the hands of the Customs men. He is the best friend I have found so far in this city.

Is it Sallafa's bleeding that worries her now? I feel sorry for women. Sometimes they get raped. Sometimes they have to bear children. And blood runs from them for several days each month. Perhaps she is thinking about Bouchra, who still has not come back. It could be. El Kebdani was right about Sallafa and Bouchra; Bouchra is the point where Sallafa's strange sadness begins. I wonder what will happen if Bouchra stays away much longer. I am certain it is not Qaabil who preoccupies her thoughts, and I feel a sudden surge of warmth towards her. It would be good to ask her forgiveness, but I do not dare. I turned and looked at her: she was totally immersed in her reverie. I liked to see her in this sad state. Never before had I seen her give in to her melancholy in this way. She has let something go inside her, and now it is lost. Perhaps she is thinking that it is lost for ever, or she may be trying to devise a way of getting it back. It would be better to go out and leave her to herself. The world is sad and decayed.

I stood up.

I'm going out to see what it looks like in the town. I haven't seen it since the day of the trouble.

She glanced up at me for an instant, surprised. Then she bowed her head, as if she could not bear to be separated from her obsession. She remained staring into emptiness while I stood there in front of her.

After a moment she raised her head and focused her eyes on mine. Did Qaabil pay you for your work last night? she asked me.

No. He hasn't paid me yet.

Wait a minute. She got up and went into the bedroom. Until now I had not seen her behave in this serious, adult manner. Today she looks like Bouchra. It was unusual for her to have mentioned Qaabil's name and not have followed it up with an insult. She will say of him: I know that pimp. I understand that rotten mind.

Surely she has a surprise for me, I thought. What can it be? As I waited I grew more impatient. She came out carrying three watches in one hand and two hundred-peseta notes in the other. I stared at the pretty blue foulard she had just wound around her head. Now she looked like an ancient Egyptian queen whose picture I had once cut out of a magazine. I went on looking at her in astonishment.

Here. Take these things. Sell the watches and keep the money you get for them. But don't mention it to anybody. And when you sell the watches be sure Qaabil doesn't find out about it. Smuggling's not regular work, and it doesn't go on long.

Her way of speaking amazed me. The words I meant to say flew off before I could say them. I took the watches and the banknotes, and stored them in various pockets of my jacket and trousers. I looked at the key in the door, and said: Are you going to lock the door from the inside?

Yes.

I opened the door and went out. After a few steps I turned around. She was standing in the doorway sobbing and wiping her eyes. I stopped walking. The feeling came over me that she was saying goodbye to me. I would have sworn that she was taking leave of me for the last time. I may never see her again. The girl in Aïn Ketiout, Asiya, Fatima, did I ever see any of them again once they had gone? I started to walk again. It was impossible to go back. My eyes filled with tears. I could not stop them from forming. I was certain that she still stood in the doorway watching me as I walked away. The force that keeps me from turning around and going back must be the same force that makes her remain standing in the doorway, unable to come after me. I am leaving the shack for good. A part of my life is ending, and another part will begin. Perhaps I shall never see any of them from the shack again.

# *11*

I was sitting with Laila Bouwala in her room. Sometimes Lalla Zehor, the proprietor of the house, served us herself. Ever since I had left the shack, I had been spending my time drinking. There is a continuous babble of girls' voices coming up from downstairs. During the past two nights I have slept with three of the girls. The only one of those whom I like is Rachida, who squirms in bed like a snake. Tonight here I am with Laila Bouwala. Hamid Zailachi told me that sometimes she wets her bed. He says it happened once when he was spending the night with her. I'm going to stay in her bed all night and see if she does it with me.

She poured what was left of the wine into the two glasses. Are we going to have another bottle, or will this be enough?

Without reflecting, I said: We'll order another. And another, and another, until we're drunk.

She got up and went to the door. She pulled the curtain aside and pushed the door, which was ajar. Then she called into the corridor: Lalla Zehor! *Agi!* She let go of the curtain and turned back to me.

What's the matter with you? she said. You look sad. Has something happened? Or don't you like being with me?

I looked at her and smiled. I'm not sad. I'm just thinking of something.

Thinking of what? She sat down smiling and lighted a cigarette, which she then put between my lips. This made me think of Sallafa. I studied Laila's figure. It is fuller and better than Sallafa's. She has long, smooth black hair. I intend to spread it over me like a blanket. I continued to run my eyes over her body.

Why are you staring at me that way? Don't you like the way I look?

I told you I was thinking of something.

Well, stop thinking about it now. It makes you look sad.

Lalla Zehor spoke outside the door: Here I am.

Come in, Lalla Zehor, Laila told her.

She walked into the room, bringing a strong wave of perfume with her. I'm here, she said.

Bring us another bottle, said Laila.

I'm going to sleep here with Laila, I told Lalla Zehor. How much is she?

Just give me sixty pesetas, and it'll be all right, she said. Nobody else would get her under a hundred.

I handed her the sixty pesetas, and twenty for the new bottle. A girl was calling up the stairs: Lalla Zehor!

I'm coming, she answered. And turning to us: What a loud voice that Rachida has! I'll send the bottle up by her, or else by Alioua Larossia.

There was the sound of footsteps, and then came two knocks on the door.

Who is it? cried Lalla Zehor.

I recognized the voice. It's me. Can I come in?

Lalla Zehor raised the curtain, and Kandoussi walked in.

We're in luck, Lalla Zehor cried. So it's you? I feel better just looking at you. Where have you been all this time? You haven't been back to see us in I don't know how long.

I was surprised to see Kandoussi.

So this is where you've been hiding out, he said to me. I've been looking everywhere, trying to find you. Come on. Get up.

But Si Kandoussi, aren't you going to sit down with us?

Lalla Zehor was always hospitable. At least have something to drink.

You'll have to excuse me, he said. I can't tonight. Some other time, *insha'Allah*.

I stood up.

Will you be back? Lalla Zehor asked me.

Of course I'll be back, I said immediately. Haven't I already paid you for the night with Laila?

If the door's locked, just knock, she said.

Now Laila spoke up. What time are you coming back? I looked at Kandoussi, and he answered for me: He'll be back whenever he wants to come back. If he's late, go to bed. But by yourself, and not with some other client.

Laila smiled. Lalla Zehor said to Kandoussi: Don't worry about your friend. I haven't got seven faces. Just the same face for everyone.

Kandoussi and I went downstairs, leaving Lalla Zehor with Laila. On the way down I asked him: Where's el Kebdani?

This is not the place to talk, he said. I'll tell you all about it when we get outside.

Going through the alleys of Bencharqi we ran into a good many drunks. From time to time Kandoussi stopped to shake someone's hand. He seemed to know great numbers of people, and they all looked glad to see him and treated him with a special respect. We said nothing to one another as we walked along. He spoke when we got to the Zoco Chico.

What café do you want to sit in? The Fuentes? The Central? The Española?

Wherever you like.

We went into the Café Central. Before we sat down we ordered a cognac and a gin. We chose a free corner. Then he said: But where have you been? I looked everywhere.

Here in Tangier. Where did you think?

I mean, where do you sleep?

I found a place in the Casbah, in Derb ben Abbou.

Is it the house next to the school?

Exactly. That's it.

You're living in a nest of thieves and whores, you know.

But they asked for papers at all the other hotels. And I've got nothing.

Fine. We'll talk about that later, he said.

The waiter came up and poured our drinks for us. After he had gone away, Kandoussi resumed talking.

Poor Kebdani. He's dead.

My eyes and mouth opened wide. Dead? I repeated weakly.

Yes, he said. He's dead. *Allah irhamou*. May Allah see to it that we all die as Moslems.

I emptied my glass and called the waiter. Then I lit a cigarette. Kandoussi drank what was in his glass.

Another round? the waiter asked.

Bring a full bottle of cognac, I told him.

Right, said Kandoussi. Bring a bottle, and I'll drink that.

But how did he die? I said.

When he rowed back to the ship it wasn't there. They'd caught sight of a Customs boat coming their way, and had to get out. He had to row ashore. The rowboat must have been thrown against a rock. They found him and the pieces of the boat lying on the beach. Poor Kebdani!

That was the death written for him, said Kandoussi.

Yes, I said sadly. You're right. It was written that way. But it's not right.

Poor Kebdani.

The waiter brought a bottle of Terry and opened it at the table. He filled the glasses, set the bottle on the table, and went away.

The only things that can happen are those Allah decides must happen, said Kandoussi.

And Qaabil?

He's been arrested.

Arrested? For what?

They're trying to connect him with Kebdani's accident. They know Kebdani worked for him.

Did they take the ship? I asked him.

No. They stopped it and went aboard and searched it.

Then they let it go.

Where's Qaabil now?

The secret police have him.

What has he told them?

So far he hasn't admitted to anything.

I finished my glass and refilled it.

You're going to be drunk fast if you go on like that, he said.

I could drink this whole bottle without moving it from my lips, I bragged. And I put my hand on the bottle. You want me to show you?

Kandoussi also put his hand on the bottle. No! Don't be crazy. I know you could drink it. Tell me: why did you leave the key with Sallafa?

She asked me for it. Naturally I let her have it. She's the one who ran the shack.

I know that. But she's run away.

Run away?

She took everything she could carry with her out of the place, and disappeared.

Where to?

How should I know? It's a safe guess she's left Tangier.

So she's gone, I said to myself.

It always ends that way if you let a whore into your life, he said.

And Bouchra? Hasn't she come back yet?

She must have gone with Sallafa. They've never been separated, not since they were kids down in Dar el Baroud.

They've gone together to Casablanca, I thought. I looked out into the Zoco Chico, full of drunks wandering up and down, and said: Well, things are back the way they were before the trouble.

Things aren't good, though, anywhere in Morocco, said Kandoussi. We're going to see much bigger trouble than that before too long. They're going to be demanding independence.

El Kebdani told me that only six funeral processions went to the mosque, and everybody knows that dozens were killed.

A lot of bodies are beginning to be washed up along the shore, he said.

I see. They threw them into the ocean afterwards.

They say that even live people got thrown in, sewn up in sacks. And some of the dead bodies had no bullets in them or any marks on them. They found one boy on the beach at Larache, with handcuffs still on his wrists. But no marks on his body anywhere.

Very bad, I said.

They'll probably keep coming across bodies for a long time. But you can never get to the bottom of all that. I have five hundred pesetas for you. Your wages for the work you did the other night. I was going to pay you tonight, but I think tomorrow would be better, now that I see how you are tonight.

Whenever, I said. It doesn't matter.

I'm going to leave the money with Sidi Mustafa at the Café Raqassa. He's reliable. Do you know him?

Yes. I go there often.

He's taking care of me, I thought. He doesn't want me to spend the money tonight.

I've got something else to say to you.

What's that?

You're not to tell anybody that you've worked for me. The other three *cargadores* who worked with us are all reliable. There's nothing to worry about there. But you never know what can happen. If they should arrest you and begin asking questions, deny everything. They may beat you, but hold on, and don't be afraid of them.

Don't worry about me.

There's one good thing, at least. You're not known as a *cargador*.

Wouldn't Qaabil tell them everything if they tortured him?

I don't think he would. But who knows? They've certainly tortured him by now.

Is the stuff in a safe place? I asked him.

We delivered it to the Hindu the same morning.

I nodded my head. I see.

You'd better sleep at your hotel tonight. But look for another place to stay. I'll find you a place that won't cost you more than fifty pesetas a month.

Who's staying at the shack now?

Nobody. Sallafa left the key at the *baqal* Qaabil always used. That shack is no good to anybody now he's in jail.

You mean the police are watching it?

They may be.

We got up. The bottle was still half full.

Would it be all right if I took it with me? I asked him.

Take it. But be sure you don't go back to see Laila.

Do you think I'm crazy? I'm tired. I'm going to sleep.

You're still young, and Allah's days are long, said Kandoussi.

I went outside to wait for him while he paid the waiter. He came out. We shook hands.

Can you get to your hotel all right? he said.

Of course. You think I'm two years old?

Remember. Don't go back to the whorehouse.

No. I told you, I'm not crazy.

I walked down the Calle del Comercio. In the alleys on each side there were drunks and whores standing around. It was about twelve o'clock, and I myself was drunk. I staggered along, feeling well able to protect myself if anyone should attack me.

On my way up the steps at Djenane el Kaptane I came face to face with a young man who was very drunk. There was no one else in the street. He turned as I brushed past him.

Where are you off to, handsome?

What do you care where I'm going?

He put his hand on the bottle I was carrying. Can't we go and drink this together?

Take your hand off the bottle, I said. Get out of here.

I stepped aside and started ahead, but he blocked my way. I live near her. In Derb Zeynana. Come on. We'll stay together all night.

What do you want of me? I cried angrily.

Why are you so skittish, gazelle? he murmured close to my ear, trying at the same time to stroke my face.

Get out of here! I shouted. What do you want?

You still don't know what I want of you? he said, leering. I want you, that's all. Come on. Spend the night with me.

I gripped the bottle by its neck. Go and spend the night with your mother or your sister, I told him.

You're talking about my mother, you little *maricón*? he roared. Insulting my mother? I'll fix you!

I backed up a bit, and he followed. Then he kicked me in the groin. I bent forward, clutching myself with both hands, while stars of pain flashed in front of my eyes. He kicked me again in the same spot. I fell and rolled down a few steps. The bottle smashed, but I went on holding the neck in my hand. He kicked again, and I ducked so he would not hit my face. His foot hit my hand instead. He went on kicking with both feet, furiously, while I made every effort to see that he did not get my face.

A girl's voice came from a nearby window: That's enough! Leave him alone! Don't kick him like that. He's younger than you.

I am trying to grab him by the leg. I duck one of his more vicious kicks, and at that moment he loses his balance and falls backwards onto the pavement. I made a great effort and got to my feet. Then I kicked him in the face.

I heard the girl's voice again. Stop it! You're going to kill each other!

He had his face covered. I went on kicking him. When I was tired of kicking, I used the broken neck of the bottle on the two hands that were spread over his face. He was bellowing like a beast. My face! My neck!

I ran on and left him there yelling. The girl's voice cried: That's what you wanted, you two. You've finally got it.

I fell several times as I ran up the stairs. Blood ran from my face, my knees, and from the hand that had held the bottle. I could still hear him bellowing as I went through the arch of Bab el Assa. I took out my handkerchief and put it to my nose. Blood was coming from my mouth as well.

At the entrance of Derb ben Abbou I stumbled on one of the steps and fell, letting go of the handkerchief as well as the broken neck of the bottle, which I still had in my hand. It took my last remaining strength to get to the hotel door. The window was open and the light was on. I called hoarsely: Zailachi! Come down quick!

From the window above he leaned out. With him were Naima and Faouziya.

Mohamed! What's the matter?

Come down.

A moment later the door opened, and he stood there barefoot and with a knife in his hand. What's happened?

I wiped the blood from my face with the sleeve of my jacket. I got into a fight with a drunk, I said. I think he's still after me.

BouChta leaned out of the window. What is it? he said. I'm coming down.

Come down fast, you pimp, said Zailachi. Then he said to me: Come on. Follow me. Was he by himself?

I spat out some blood. Yes. He was alone, the son of a whore.

Hurry up.

I slipped again in the street, trying to follow him. Where the alley turned he slowed down. Then he stopped, and peered cautiously around the corner. After that he began to run again, and stopped only at the entrance to the Place de la Casbah.

Where was he?

On the stairs of Djenane el Kaptane, I said.

BouChta caught up with us. He too was barefoot, and he carried a club.

We did not find him. The same girl was still in the window. He's gone, she said. And you go away too. Be sensible. Do you want to wake up the whole neighbourhood?

She was right. Already a good many men and women were

leaning out of the windows and bending over the balcony railings, to see what was going on. There was a pool of blood in the place where I had left him. We followed the trail of blood down the steps for several metres, until it suddenly ended.

Where'd he go? mused Zailachi.

Come on. Let's go back. He's gone, I said.

Lucky for him he got away.

Going back up to the hotel I told them the whole story, from the moment he had blocked my passage to the point when I cut him with the bottle and began to run.

BouChta walked along beside us, saying nothing. I knew he was the sort who would not even dare disturb a sitting hen, but in spite of that, his presence made us feel better, more ready to deal with whatever trouble might present itself.

Do you know that girl who was talking in the window? Zailachi asked me.

No, I said. Who is she?

Her name is Fatiha Cherifa. Her husband was a policeman who got tuberculosis and tried to cure himself at home. He had a friend who used to go and visit him, and it seems the friend used to smoke *kif* and get drunk with the policeman's wife. Sometimes the man with tuberculosis would take a chance and smoke and drink with them, and half the time ended up vomiting blood. I think he knew his wife was playing with the other man, but he was patient. One night they drank more than usual, and the friend began to pay attention to her right in front of him. He went at the friend with a knife, but the friend pulled out his pistol and shot him.

He stopped talking.

Did it kill him? I asked.

He died when he got to the hospital.

What about her? What did they do to her?

What would they do? They questioned her and let her go.

BouChta spoke up. When women and love get mixed up, the story is always dirty.

She's got two baby girls, said Zailachi. The Missionaries

adopted her when she was little, and made a nurse out of her. She speaks three foreign languages. But her greatest talent is right between her legs, like all other women.

Naima Mesrara and Faouziya Achaqa were leaning out of the window above our heads. Naima, open the door, said Zailachi.

Push on it. It's open.

There was talking and laughing inside. On the second and third floors some of the roomers were still up and around. The night-watchman came out of one of the second-floor rooms, a cigarette hanging from his lips. He must have been having a drink with the people who lived in that room.

Everything all right? he asked us.

Zailachi said: Yes.

We went upstairs, and he stood looking after us. Our room had been a very large one. The proprietor had made three rooms out of it by erecting partitions. It was my section where everyone liked to gather at night. They sat there even when I was not at home, because it was the only one of the three rooms that had a window in it. The window looked out into the alley of Derb ben Abbou.

Faouziya, go down to the kitchen and put some water on to boil, said BouChta. At that moment Zailachi noticed the rip in my trousers at the knee.

Come into the other room with me, he told me.

We went into his room. He took a pair of flannel trousers from his bag and held them out to me. Wait until Faouziya comes and washes your cuts, he said.

I told him to bring me a glass of cognac. He went back into my room. The door into the corridor opened, and Faouziya came in carrying the tea-kettle.

Here's the cognac, said Naima.

Take off your clothes to wash, Faouziya told me. Are you afraid of us?

I took my jacket and trousers off in front of them both, and stood in my underwear. My left elbow was skinned and bleeding. I let the two girls rub my wounds with hot water and cognac.

Zailachi was busy opening another bottle of cognac. Suddenly there was a loud knocking on the door. I started to get up to open it. The girls had finished taking care of me.

Stay where you are, said Zailachi. He set down the bottle and rose. The knocking went on, very loud.

Who is it? said Zailachi.

A hoarse voice cried: Open the door!

Naima and Faouziya grew pale. The police! murmured Naima. Only the police knock like that. They're the only ones who ever pound that way.

Hide the bottle somewhere, said BouChta.

I was sitting on the couch. I reached out and took the bottle. I sat there holding it. Then I got up and looked out of the window. Two policemen in uniform stood in front of the entrance door downstairs.

Zailachi opened the door, and we saw two secret policemen standing there.

What took you so long? Why didn't you open up? one of them said. Well, say something.

He slapped Zailachi. The two came into the room. I still held the bottle in my hand.

Girls and liquor, is that it? Give me that bottle.

I handed it to him. He looked at it.

So you drink Terry, do you? Your papers.

I have no papers.

He turned to BouChta. And you?

BouChta took out his identity card and handed it to him. The man glanced at it and slipped it into his pocket. Then he turned to the two girls and said: Put on your *djellabas*. Quick!

The other one handcuffed Zailachi and me together.

We all went downstairs to the first floor, where we found three young men and two girls with another secret policeman. Two of the young men were handcuffed together, and the third had them hanging from one hand. The officer shut the open handcuff on BouChta's wrist. The four girls walked out first and the rest of us followed. When we were outside, the police pointed in the direction of the Place de la Casbah, saying: That way.

Two of the youths were whispering behind us. No talking! yelled a policeman.

There were two jeeps in the Place de la Casbah. The girls got into one, and we got into the other.

They've caught a lot of game this time, I thought.

We were sitting very close together in the jeep. When we got to the Souq ez Zra, the other car continued down towards the Zoco de Fuera. Ours stopped there at the Brigada Criminal. There in an office they searched us one by one, taking away our belts, shoestrings and money. All they left us was our cigarettes and matches. One of the three other youths had a small knife in his pocket.

What's this supposed to be for? asked the policeman who was searching him. No? All right, we'll see about that later.

After they had taken down our names they turned us over to a man with keys in his hand. Zailachi and I followed him down a narrow corridor until he stopped in front of a door. As he was opening it, one of the men who had brought us in the jeep came up. He pushed us through a doorway into a room where a light bulb hung down from the ceiling. Three other prisoners sat in the room, but one of them was asleep. The policeman unfastened the handcuffs, stepped outside, and slammed the door.

Everything they do here is part of the punishment, I thought. My left wrist hurt a little, and I rubbed it. I looked at the door that was reinforced with metal plates, and reflected that this door was stronger than any of the doors that had shut me in before. The doors are getting tighter. Here I am, finally, in a real prison. Zailachi sat down on the floor with his arms on his knees. Sit down, he said.

I sat beside him facing the two young men who were awake. The floor was cold as ice. Great spots of dampness covered the walls and ceiling. In one corner of the room was a latrine hole with a water tap directly above it. Whatever they give you here they give in a way that makes it all a part of the punishment, I thought. I glanced at the hole in the corner. The stench that came up from it made me feel sick to my stomach. Zailachi brought out a pack of cigarettes and passed it around. The one who was sleeping sat bent over with his head resting on his folded arms.

Zailachi pointed in his direction. What's the matter with him? he asked the others.

He's drunk.

He's better off like that, in this cold, said Zailachi.

The two young men were shivering.

How long have you been in here? Zailachi asked them.

The same one who had spoken before answered now. They arrested us this afternoon. We were playing cards in the Café Debbou.

The other one smoked silently, looked at the floor. He raised his head only to take a long pull on his cigarette from time to time. Then later, his head down, he would exhale, and the smoke would look like someone's breath on a cold morning.

# 12

By the time morning came, we were all shivering with the cold. Each time one of us got up to use the latrine the others crouched further forward, staring at the floor. And the smell grew worse. The young man who had been asleep during the night drank a great deal of water, the same as Zailachi and I. It was the great thirst of the morning after drinking. Zailachi stood up and began to do exercises. He was in a good mood.

Get up and do this if you want to get warm, he told me.

No, I said.

Each time he made a vigorous gesture the others glanced up. I watched him during the entire time he did his gymnastics.

Get up! he said. What's the matter with you? There's nothing better if you want to stop feeling the cold.

The cuts on my knee and my elbow hurt. They'll begin to bleed again if I start doing that.

He did not say any more. He was beginning to pant, and his motions were growing slower. He walked over to the latrine hole and spat into it. He turned on the water tap and washed his hands and face, wetting his hair and smoothing it back. He squatted, urinated, washed his sex, and then washed the hand that had washed the sex. He drank a little more water and came back to sit in his place on the floor with his hands on his knees. Drops of water ran from his chin and from the tips of his fingers. He bent his head forward. Little by little he began to breathe normally. Then he raised his head towards me. We looked at each other smiling for a moment, and then he burst out laughing. This made me laugh too.

The sons of whores! he said. They caught us the way a cat catches a mouse.

Where do you think they've taken the girls? I said.

The Zoco Chico police station. Where else would they take them?

Do you think it will be a morals charge? I asked him.

I don't believe so. We weren't making any trouble. They found us drinking with two whores, that's all.

How many days do you think they'll keep us here?

Not later than Monday or Tuesday, he said. Today's Saturday. After a pause he went on: You're lucky. BouChta too. He's just a tailor.

I'm lucky? I cried, astonished.

Yes. You've never been convicted of anything. You've never been in jail. But I have, and they may accuse me of a new robbery or something.

I wonder why they didn't put BouChta in here with us, I said.

They just didn't happen to. I don't think there's any reason. They'll let him out too on Monday or Tuesday.

You think they're going to let BouChta and me off that easily?

You'll see, he said.

And Naima and Faouziya? I said after a moment.

They'll be out drinking and whoring again on Monday or Tuesday. The worst that can happen to them is that they might make them go into a whorehouse to work, where they can give them a medical examination every week. Anyway, I think BouChta and Faouziya will be getting married as soon as they get out of here.

You mean he's in love with her?

I don't know. But he wants to live with her.

And you?

What do you mean, and me?

I mean you and Naima, I said.

He put his forefinger to his temple and drew circles with it. Are you out of your mind? She's like every other whore I ever knew. I didn't come into this world to marry a whore.

I heard the sound of footsteps close by, outside the door. We all turned in that direction. The little square window in the middle of the door opened. Then the door swung inward rapidly, making a great noise.

They do it that way to scare us, I thought. Even the way they open the door is part of the punishment.

Two old men came in, one of them carrying a large tea-kettle and a basket full of metal mugs to drink out of, and the other a white canvas sack. They said good morning. Behind them in the corridor stood two guards. They gave each of us a loaf of bread and a mug of tea.

You've got fifteen minutes before they take out the mugs, said one of the guards.

The two old men went out and the guards shut the door. The little window remained open. Both the tea and the bread were hot. We ate and drank without speaking.

Leave half your bread for the afternoon, Zailachi advised me. They won't bring anything around again until this time tomorrow.

I nodded my head. After we had finished, Zailachi pulled out a cigarette and passed it to the others. He and I shared a second cigarette between us. I noticed that the two youths who had been arrested in the Café Debbou left none of their bread for later. The third one, like Zailachi and me, saved the greater part of his. Always when I have drunk and smoked a great deal, the following day thirst takes the place of appetite.

We continued to smoke in silence, sipping what was left of the tea. My body had begun to glow with warmth. The little window stayed open. It may be because of the window that we remain so quiet. What would life be like, I wondered, if all of it had to be spent sitting like this here in this room? We would all have to exist only in our memories, acting out the parts we play here until we were so bored by both them and the memories that we came to rest in a silence like this one. We would disappear one by one, until all of us were gone, and the unluckiest of us would be the one who disappeared last. I prefer to be with people, even though they may be my enemies. I would rather be shut up in a place like this with others than be free and solitary. It would be better to be the first rather than the last to disappear.

The door opened, and the old man who had brought the tea came in. A guard stood behind him watching us. We finished off the last drops quickly, and dropped the mugs into the old man's basket, on top of those that were already there, and we thanked him.

May Allah forgive you and us both, he said.

Some of us answered: *Amin.*

The guard slammed shut both the little window and the door. The violent sounds were no longer producing their effect. I had become indifferent to them. With time I should not even notice them, and perhaps not even notice the fact that I was shut into a room. But I am still not used to solitude.

Zailachi took out a small pencil and set to work writing on the wall.

What are you writing? I asked him.

I'm writing two lines of a poem by Abou el Qacem Chabbi. He was from Tunis.

And what did he say?

Here's what he says:

> *If some day the people decide to live, fate must bend to*
> *    that desire*
> *There will be no more night when the chains have broken.*

Do you understand?

No, but it's magnificent. What does it mean?

He's talking about the desire to live.

And what does the desire to live mean?

It means that if a man or a country is enslaved and decides to try and get free, Allah will help. He says: *the dawn will respond and the chains will break* because men will make it happen.

I see.

Abou el Qacem Chabbi was a great poet, he said. The others were listening attentively.

You're lucky, I said to Zailachi.

Lucky? Me? He was surprised.

Yes. You're lucky.

Why?

Because you know how to read and write.

So I can read and write, he said. What good is it? Here I am in this room. Who knows what they're going to accuse me of? Things I've done? Things I haven't done?

He began again to write on the wall, asking me at the same time as he formed the first letter: What's this?

I don't know.

It's *alif*, he said. Then he made another letter. And this?

I don't know. What is it?

That's *ba*. And this?

*Tsa*, I said.

How do you happen to know that one?

Because I've always heard people say: *alif, el ba, et tsa.* And I repeated with him the reading of the three letters.

We can make words out of these three letters, like *aboun, baboun, bata, taba.*

He stepped away from the wall. Some day I'll teach you to read and write, he said. You could learn easily.

Do you think it's easy?

Why not? Aren't you a man?

I asked him to repeat the verses by the Tunisian poet several times, until I had learned them by heart.

During the afternoon the young man who had been asleep the night before began to pace restlessly, from one end of the room to the other. The rest of us sat quietly, watching him. At one point he seized the piece of bread he had saved from the morning, walked over to the latrine, and crumbled it in his hands, dropping the pieces down the hole. I looked at Zailachi.

It's his business, he whispered. Let him do what he likes with the bread.

The other two glared angrily at the youth. It seemed to me that if he made one more move, there might easily be a fight.

Why'd you throw the bread down the hole? one of them demanded.

I can do what I want with my bread, he said, glowering.

But you threw away bread, *en neama d'Allah!*

I tell you I'm free! the other cried.

You're a pile of shit!

I'm free to do as I like with my bread, and with myself, too!

Yes, but do it when you're alone.

Suddenly the young man began to pound the wall with his fists, and soon he was butting it with his head. After a few blows he slid to the floor unconscious, his hands and forehead running with blood. Zailachi rose and knocked loudly on the door. The little window opened and a guard said: What is it?

Somebody hurt himself, Zailachi said. He came back and sat down. That's all we can do, he whispered.

The young man who had been objecting now said: That's what he gets for doing what he did.

The door opened and two secret policemen entered, accompanied by the uniformed guard. What's going on in here?

He crumbled up his bread and threw it down the latrine, Zailachi said. And then he started to hit the wall.

And before that, what happened? asked the other secret policeman.

Nothing.

You didn't quarrel first?

Zailachi looked around at all of us.

No, he said. Ask him when he comes to.

One of the policemen walked over and examined the blood stains on the wall. We'll see later whether there wasn't some sort of trouble here before he began to hit himself, he said.

The youth lay quite still, with the blood coming out slowly from his cuts. The men went out and shut the door, leaving the window open.

A quarter of an hour later they came back, bringing two attendants with a stretcher. They lifted the young man onto the canvas and carried him out, still unconscious. There were puddles and smears of blood where he had lain. Again the door shut and the window remained open.

There must be something the matter with him, I said.

Let him do what he likes, said Zailachi. He's either an alcoholic or he smokes too much *kif*.

The young man who had been critical added: Or Allah has put a curse on him. Or his father has.

Of course, said the other. You get punished for whatever you do.

We were silent. Our cigarettes had given out. The butts we had thrown away were extremely short. I picked one up, however, and smoked it.

We awoke Monday morning completely exhausted. The two others merely sat, bent over, and Zailachi did not do his morning exercises. In spite of the ugly grey pallor his dark skin had taken on as a result of hunger, he seemed in better condition than the rest of us. I felt only like vomiting, and I was certain that I should, if anyone used the latrine. I thought of that noon I had spent on the docks, when the idea of bread mixed with excrement first flowered in my mind.

The guard threw open the door and called out my name. I stood up, and found that I was dizzy and that my knees were trembling. I said goodbye, even though I had no idea whether I was going to be let out or not. I went along with the guard, and as I climbed the stairs my laceless shoes flapped. Being out of that hateful cell was like being half-free. We went into a room where a large camera was set up in the centre, with a chair in front of it. The guard withdrew, and the photographer told me to sit down. The room was heated. To remember the cell was like remembering being shut into a refrigerator. The man came over to me and arranged my pose. Then he went behind the camera and told me to look into the lens. He took one full-face picture and two profiles. This must be for their records, I thought. He asked my name, and showed me how to push my fingers, one by one, onto the ink-pad and make their marks on a piece of white paper.

A secret policeman entered and began to speak in French and Spanish with the photographer, who was a Moroccan. When the work was finished, the photographer ran his eyes over the paper and asked me if I knew how to sign it. I said no.

Most of them are like that, said the policeman.

Of course, the photographer said.

Next they asked me to push my thumb again into the ink-pad, and make my sign with it at the bottom of the paper. I did not dare ask them what was written on the paper, but I did tell them that I had done nothing.

I have nothing to do with that, said the photographer. Now go down and report to the guard who brought you up here.

Then the secret policeman, speaking in Spanish, asked me what kind of work I did. I told him I had no work.

And so what do you live on, if you have no work?

I don't know. I just live. I do whatever work I can find, wherever I find it.

I see, he said. Well, go on downstairs.

I left them talking together, and went out, shuffling in my open shoes. On the floor below I looked in vain for the guard. I stood in the corridor, with the door into the street open before me. I could see the people going past. Two men dressed in civilian clothes entered and walked in front of me. Secret policemen, I supposed. Zailachi was right when he said they would release me on Monday or Tuesday. It looks as if it were going to be today. A guard came out of an office.

Have you finished with the photographer? he asked me.

Yes.

Come with me. He took me into his office. There were two other men inside, both dressed in civilian clothes. They had me put my thumb-print on another sheet of paper covered with words. I told them my name and they gave me back my money, belt and shoe-laces.

I wondered what they had written about me on this piece of paper. They can write whatever they want, since I have no idea what the ink marks mean. Nor do I dare ask them to bring someone who will read it to me before I sign it.

Get out of here, said one of the secret policemen.

I turned and stepped out of the office, having completely forgotten my fatigue and my nausea. As I went through the doorway I ran into a man wearing civilian clothing, and excused myself. He shoved me violently aside, so that I hit the wall.

Look where you're going, you halfwit! he said. He went on, and I stooped to pick up one of my shoes, which had fallen off.

He must be a policeman. Only a policeman could behave like that.

When I got into the street I put the laces into my shoes and attached my belt to my trousers. It was a clear cold day with a bright sun overhead, and I breathed deeply as I walked along.

I went into Harouch's restaurant in the Zoco de Fuera. He sold bean soup. I was thinking about the money Kandoussi had said he would leave for me with the owner of the Café Raqassa. And I also was casting about in my head for an idea for some sort of work. I must find a new way to live.

# 13

The alarm clock began to ring. I reached out into the darkness and shut it off. Then I got up and turned on the light. It was five o'clock. I could feel sleep still hanging there deliciously close, just inside my eyes. The boat will come into port in an hour, I was thinking. I glanced at Naima. She was sleeping quietly. I hate to live with a girl who never works. All she ever has to do is open her legs, to me or someone else. Does she expect me to marry her, the way BouChta did Faouziya? I haven't gone that crazy yet.

I dressed rapidly, picked up the market basket, and snapped off the light. Then I went softly out of the room. Downstairs I washed my face in water that was like melted snow. I was careful when I woke the night watchman. He began to pummel the air with his fists, as he always did when anyone woke him, and then he stared wildly at me, saying nothing.

Abdeslam! I said. It's Choukri. I want to go out.

He gave a great sigh and got wearily out of bed. I followed him to the front door of the hotel. As I went out, he said: May Allah be kind to you this morning. I nodded at him and went down the silent alley. The day was violet-coloured now. The signs of poverty, blotted out by night, were becoming visible once again. The lucky ones are at home in bed at this hour. They don't get up to work. They lie there, comfortable as excrement enfolded in the belly. There are many things for them to rely upon: Allah, their own personalities, love, power. But I can rely only upon my own health and the fact that I am young.

I stopped just inside Bab el Assa and looked out over the harbour. I could see that the water was rough.

When I got down to the waterfront I found Boussouf standing by a kiosk having a bowl of bean soup. I said hello, and ordered a bowl for myself. Between us we arranged the price. He would do the work for me for three thousand francs.

I heard yesterday that the steerage is going to be full of Jews on their way to Palestine, said Boussouf.

I'm more interested in the French and Senegalese soldiers on their way to Algeria, I told him. They don't bargain so much. But Jews! Most of them are businessmen themselves. Even the ones who aren't know just how much everything is worth.

But they're leaving Morocco for good, and they'll be sure to want souvenirs from the last port of call.

We'll see.

We walked out onto the breakwater and got into the rowboat. He began to row slowly. Watching the oars cut the water put me in mind of the time when I had been working in the vineyard at Oran with the old man, I ploughing the earth, he yelling and scolding. Come on! Watch where you're going! To the left, you good-for-nothing Riffian! Come on! You're still half asleep! I'm going to get Monsieur Segundi to put you in the kitchen peeling potatoes. Hit the mule harder! That's all you're good for, peeling potatoes and washing dishes.

It was at this hour that we used to go out into the vineyards to work. The old man complained without stopping, and the sound of his voice made my hands tighten on the reins. If it had not been for my attack on the beautiful boy in the field, I should still be there working. I remembered my mother's face, my aunt's face. I now understand why my aunt treated me with such tenderness. She had no children of her own. And I believe it was her husband who made her send me home in order to avoid possible trouble.

Look! said Boussouf. The ship's coming into the harbour.

I'm looking, I said.

He stopped rowing, pulled one oar out of the water, and dropped the oarlock into a hole beside the plank where I sat. We began to row together.

The ship's full of soldiers, he said.

As we drew near the side of the ship a Frenchman in uniform called down to us: *Hé! Qu'est-ce que tu as là-dedans?*

I signalled to him to wait a minute. Boussouf pulled out the coil of rope and got it ready to throw.

Catch it! I shouted.

Several hands reached out to grab the end of the rope, which was weighted with knots. Boussouf tossed up the coil with force, and a black soldier caught it.

Tie it tight! I called to him in French.

Come on. Climb up! cried several soldiers.

I started to climb up the rope, hand over hand.

That's right! Keep it up! *Bravo!* Good! shouted the voices. A Senegalese soldier helped me onto the deck. Boussouf had tied the basket onto the tail end of the rope once I was aboard. I leaned over the railing and began to pull it up. Another black soldier approached me and said: What have you got for sale, brother?

Without turning my head towards him I answered: Swiss watches, shawls, Japanese handkerchiefs and cigarette-lighters.

It was a French soldier who helped me get the basket over the railing and onto the deck. *Allez! Laisse voir ce que tu as là-dedans.*

I took out the carton of watches, leaving everything else in the basket. Here are the watches, I told them.

How much is this one?

Five thousand francs.

It's not a fake?

What do you mean? I don't sell fake watches.

Three thousand.

Four thousand, I said.

No, no! I'll give you three thousand.

Take it. It's yours. I was thinking: If one of them buys something, they'll all begin.

The watches were disappearing from my hands one after the other, and my pockets were filling up with banknotes. Suddenly a soldier appeared and planted himself in front of me. Give me back my money, he said.

If I do that, I thought, they'll all start asking for their money back. I can't.

Why? I asked him.

They say your watches are no good.

Listen, I told him. Whoever told you that didn't have enough money to buy a watch, that's all.

Are you going to give me back my money?

You picked out the watch yourself. Nobody made you buy it.

Dozens of pairs of eyes were staring doubtfully at me. I heard throats being cleared. The blond French soldier spoke: Mine's all right. I'm going to keep mine.

I went quietly down to the steerage deck where the Jews were travelling. It smelled of mildew and vomit.

What have you got, boy? asked a Jewish woman in a tired voice.

Japanese shawls and handkerchiefs, I told her.

Several other women gathered around me. Let's see what you've got in your basket, the first one said.

What a pretty colour that one is! a girl exclaimed to a woman who was probably her mother. How much is this?

A thousand francs.

Seven hundred.

I was thinking: I've got to sell everything fast and get out of here.

A pot-bellied old man with a pointed grey beard suddenly cried: It's cheap material! Wash it once and the whole thing is gone. No more colour.

The woman beside him turned to him. What do you know about it? she cried. These things are for women.

I know the stuff, the old man said. The Hindus sell it wholesale all over Tangier.

It's always hard to sell to old people, I kept telling myself. They always pride themselves on knowing everything.

The Jewish women around me went on buying, without paying any more attention to the old man. From time to time he cried at them: You're crazy! You're buying the worst quality! The lowest!

The shawls and scarves were disappearing, but the sharp smell of the vomit was still there in my nostrils. There was a sudden jolt and the boat stopped moving. I pocketed the money for the last handkerchief and began working my way through the shouting women. Bring more stuff! they were crying.

As I came up on deck a Senegalese soldier some distance away caught sight of me and began to call out: Hey, you! Wait for me there!

He probably wants me to take back the watch I sold him, I thought. I hurried through the crowd to the other end of the deck.

There was a circle of soldiers around Rami. That drunken brute, who practically never gets out of his bed, must be selling them watches for half the price I charged. I went over to him.

You're the same old pimp, aren't you? I said.

Who do you think you're talking to?

You. Who did you think I was talking to?

Wait till we're in town. I'll show you, he said.

I'll spit up your ass-hole, I told him.

I could see Boussouf rowing rapidly towards the ship. I waited until he was below, and tossed the basket into the rowboat. Then I began to climb down the rope, letting myself slide as I went. The rope took the skin off the palms of my hands. As I went, the taut end of the rope above me was suddenly cut, and I fell the rest of the way, landing in the middle of the rowboat.

Pftu! cried Boussouf. This is no way to earn money. You want to break the boat?

That Senegalese son of a whore must have cut the rope, I said.

To hell with this fucking work, he went on angrily.

Row hard, I told him. They may throw things at us. It wouldn't be the first time. I know those soldiers, the sons of whores!

Look out! shouted Boussouf. He and I both ducked as a beer bottle came down at us.

Take one of the floorboards and ward them off, he told me.

I did what he suggested.

The black man was screaming insults after us, and squeezing an invisible neck between his two hands. It was as if I could feel him strangling me. Then two bottles came at once, and I parried them with the floorboard.

Ow! My hand! *Inaal dinhoum!* I threw the board far from the rowboat, and began to lick and suck my wound. It was a wound that pleased me. Not for a long time had I so enjoyed watching my blood run out. And the mixture of salt and sweet is pleasant in my mouth. But I began to feel painful pricklings in the spot on my hip where I had landed. Boussouf stopped rowing. We were far enough away from the ship now. He stood up, seized his crotch, and waved it wildly at those standing by the rail.

What's that for? I said. Who's interested in what you're doing now? The current's against us.

We began to row together.

After a moment he said: But what did you do to them?

Nothing. It's all Rami's fault.

And what did he do?

He always sells his watches at half price. The next time I see him in town I'm going to piss on him.

You didn't talk about the war in Algeria?

Of course not. Are you crazy?

And with the Jews?

No, no. Nothing. What would I tell them? Should I tell the French and Senegalese soldiers not to go to Algeria and fight? Or tell the Jews not to emigrate to Palestine?

The tide and the current were very strong, and the wind was coming up. Suddenly Boussouf's oar cracked in half. Only the handle remained.

Now we're in trouble, I said.

Pfu! All this for your three thousand francs! he cried.

It's not my fault.

The waves had begun to spill into the boat.

Listen, I said. You take care of bailing it out. I'll tie the other oar at the stern and try to steer.

The current is taking us towards El Menar. We'll hit the rocks there unless we're lucky.

We'll take care of that when we get near the shore, I said.

My whole life depends on this boat, Boussouf declared.

The current's not going to take us any farther than Villa Harris, I told him.

You're trying to tell me what the current will do around here? You don't know anything about it. But tell me this. How much are you going to pay me if my boat gets smashed up?

We'll try not to let that happen, I said.

I want to know now. How much are you going to give me?

I'll give you twice as much as we agreed on.

What? Six thousand francs?

That's right.

And for six thousand francs—

The boat tipped violently, and he fell over backwards. Quickly I brought the oar-handle down on his left shoulder, and then on his right one.

You damned coward! he roared.

Shut up, or I'll throw you in.

You'll see later.

I cupped my groin in my hand and shook the mass at him.

You'll suck this for me! I cried.

He lay back on the seat-board of the prow, without trying to get up again. I busied myself taking off my belt, and started to attach it to the oarlock at the stern. At that moment he came at me with the oar-handle. I ducked, and the oar slipped out of his hands onto the floor of the boat. We grappled, and I kneed him in the groin. Then I pushed him backwards.

I grabbed the oar-handle, and he began to yell: No! No! His eyes looked as though they would pop out of his head, and his face had turned very pale.

Sit still, or you go into the water, I told him.

The oar I had been trying to fix to the stern was now floating far behind us. Keeping the oar-handle in one hand, I began to scoop out the water with an oil can. The boat was turning round and round as it went along on the current. After a moment I tossed the can at him.

It's your turn now.

He took the can and set to work silently bailing out the water. I thought of Naima. Perhaps she is still asleep. She's up there dreaming while I'm here fighting with this bear. I don't know why I keep her with me. It's not love, that's certain. It may be just habit. Perhaps it's merely her indifference. She has no blisters on her palms, no beer bottle has hit her hand, she does not know the sweet salt taste of her blood in her mouth. When she wakes up she will wash and go downstairs in her nightgown to talk with the night-watchman or the proprietor. If one of the clients of the hotel invites her into his room I think she is not likely to refuse. She once said: The only excuse for love is marriage. I replied: I'm afraid marriage would mean the end of love. What keeps us together is the fact that neither of us belongs completely to the other. Thus there is always that element of uncertainty between us.

We were drifting nearer to the beach at Villa Harris. The waves rise and crash before rolling onto the shore. The water is full of sand. Fishermen have often assured me that sharks never go near cloudy water. We got ready to jump out. I was the first overboard. I swam underwater for as long as I could hold my breath. Then I raised my head above the water and turned. Boussouf was coming close behind me. The waves would raise me very high, and then let me drop straight down, into what seemed like an abyss. I'm carrying my death on my shoulders now, I thought. Once I had gone to visit my friend Manolo in the hospital, and he had cried out: Oh, my God! Take me out of this suffering! He had tried to commit suicide, because he had a fatal disease of the lungs. But the nuns in the hospital had managed to keep him alive.

I swallowed some water, and for an instant began to dog-paddle, as if I were swimming in a well. I got my breath back, and explored the bottom to see how deep it was. My feet touched the sand, and I stood up. A wave pounded over me. I swallowed more water. Then I ran up onto the beach.

Stand up! I yelled to Boussouf. It's shallow! I did not know whether he had heard me or not. He kept swimming until he had landed on the beach. The boat was grounded a good way down the shore.

Boussouf stood up, looked first at the boat and then at me, frowning. He's looking at me now as I were a lamb he was getting ready to roast. If I let myself be afraid of him, it'll be the end of me. If he beats me up he'll take everything I've got on me. He'll go off and leave me here naked.

He came nearer, and I backed up. Let's go and see how the boat is, I said.

He began to walk along the beach, a few steps ahead of me. The boat was touching the sand and moving with the waves. We worked a while trying to pull it further up onto the sand. It was hard work.

When we had finished, he stood looking down at it. There must be some broken places, he said.

Where? I don't see any.

I know! he cried. I know my boat!

What's the matter now? I said.

This is going to cost you ten thousand francs!

Why should it cost ten thousand francs?

Are you going to pay me or not?

No, I'm not. I told you I'd give you six thousand.

All right!

His fist hit the left side of my face, and bright lights exploded in my eyes. I backed up a few steps so as not to fall. Then he attacked like a bull. If I let him get hold of me, he's going to break my ribs, I thought, jumping out of his way, so that his attack ended in a clumsy swinging at the air. It had suddenly begun to rain, and it rained harder each second.

Come here, you son of a whore! he bellowed. Do you think you're going to catch me off my guard now? Like you did in the boat? Come on!

I kept ducking his lunges, and he continued to follow me along, shouting and gesticulating. I mustn't waste my energy, I thought. I've got to let him be the one to do the attacking.

He had begun to laugh and make gestures to entice me nearer to him, so that we would fight hand to hand. You're a coward! he yelled. But who's going to help you now?

I did not answer.

Suddenly he sprang forward and grabbed my hips. I seized his neck between my hands. Then I brought my right knee fast up to his face. He raised his head. I began to pummel his face. Suddenly he yelled and bent down. Then he fell over, holding his foot with both hands. The blood ran not only from his nose, but also from the under part of his foot. Then I saw something that glistened. It was a broken bottle buried in the sand, like an artichoke. The cut was very deep. I have no idea why it made me happy to see the blood being absorbed by the sand in the pouring rain. It made me feel that the rain itself was the sky bleeding. I thought of the sheep whose throat they had cut, back in the Rif, when they had filled a bowl with its blood and made my mother drink it. I counted out six thousand francs in wet bills, folded them, and tossed them onto the sand beside Boussouf. Then I turned and walked away. Behind me I heard him crying: Come back here, you son of a whore! Come back here and I'll spit up your ass!

As I got to the highway, I saw the bus from El Menar

coming. I began to wave, and it stopped. The rear door opened. I got in and handed a wet thousand-franc bill to the conductor.

What's the matter? he said. What happened to you?

No. Everything's all right, I said.

The passengers turned to stare at me as I went forward along the aisle. There were only seven or eight of them. I looked out of the window towards the beach. There he is, only now limping towards the rowboat.

After I got off the bus in the Zoco de Fuera I noticed many people staring at me. Two women walking under one tiny umbrella behind me were discussing me. One turned to the other. That poor boy, she said. And the other replied: Yes. What do you suppose could have happened to him?

They don't know anything, I thought. All they know is how to be sorry for people and say hard luck.

At the hotel I found the watchman in the *sala*, joking with the cleaning woman as she scrubbed the floor. She dropped her rag, and they both turned to ask me what had happened to me.

I'm all right, I said, and I went upstairs. The door of my room was open. My things were not in their regular places. The whore who's the daughter of a whore has played a good hand. Everything of any value is gone: my transistor, my alarm clock, five wrist-watches and a dozen cigarette-lighters.

I went downstairs to the *sala*. You didn't see Naima when she went out, did you? I asked.

No. Why, is something wrong?

No, nothing, I said. But I think she's gone for good, and without telling me goodbye.

But nothing happened?

I shook my head. Nothing's happened. Then I went back upstairs to change my clothes. At least she left my clothes behind. Now she'll probably begin a new life with another lover somewhere, just as she did with Hamid Zailachi and others long before that. Only a filthy whore like her could have done this. And yet, maybe it is just as well. Now I am forced to find a new pattern in my life, this one being finished.

That afternoon I went to the Café Moh. I had an Egyptian movie magazine with me, full of photographs of Arab actors and singers. I was in the habit of buying three or four of these publications each week, to look at the pictures of film stars wearing Oriental costumes. Sometimes I masturbated in front of the sexier dancing girls. Hamid Zailachi's brother Abdelmalek would read me the captions when he felt in the mood. He had left his studies in Tetuan and come to Tangier, where he did nothing but smoke *kif*, eat *majoun*, drink wine, and look for whores and occasional boys. All the other men I knew in the café were illiterate. One of them could write his name, but with great difficulty. We all considered Abdelmalek the most important habitué of the café. He reads the Arabic periodicals to us in a strong, clear voice. If an article deals with the politics of an Arab country, the owner of the café shuts off the radio, and everyone listens intently. Sometimes he would stand up, lay aside the magazine or newspaper, and launch into a speech, merely to show off his learning. I noticed that he constantly quoted the Koran and the Hadith. Often one of us would interrupt him and ask for a clearer explanation. These were occasions for him to hold his knowledge over our heads, and he would make his explanation still more obscure. While he spoke, someone would hand him a pipe of *kif*. He would stop talking for a moment while he smoked, reach down to the table from where he stood and take a few sips of tea, and then continue from where he had left off. When he finished speaking, most of the men would congratulate him on his performance, and the owner of the café would hand him another glass of tea and some bread and butter. Some nights I invited him to eat with me in one of the restaurants. Afterwards we would go to a bar in the Zoco Chico to get drunk, or go and spend the night together with two whores in a brothel. I was very proud to appear in public with him.

That afternoon he was sitting with Grida, Mesari, and old Afiouna, who supplied the *kif* and *majoun* to the café. I asked for a glass of black coffee and bought five pesetas' worth of *kif* from Afiouna. They were discussing King Farouk, Mohamed Neguib, and the actions of Gamal Abd el Nasser in the July Twenty-Third Revolution. I was interested. I smoked a pipe of *kif*, and filled another which I offered to Grida. He refused it. I held it out to Abdelmalek. He did not take it either.

Put your *kif* away, he told me. We've got plenty of our own.

We want to talk quietly now, without being interrupted, Mesari added.

I saw that they were excluding me from their company. The *qahouaji* set a glass of coffee on the table. I asked Afiouna to sell me two pieces of *majoun*, which I ate as I sipped the hot coffee.

Kemal the Turk came through the door, drunk. I tried to get him to sit with me, but he refused. Then he leaned over and whispered in French into my ear: I've got half a bottle of whisky. I'm going up onto the roof. Do you want a drink?

You go up first, so Moh won't notice.

I continued to sip my coffee for a while after he had gone on. Then, taking the glass of coffee and the pipe with me, I climbed the stairs. I found him drinking out of the bottle.

Ah! Fill the *sebsi* for me, he said. I handed him the pipe and the *kif* so he could fill it himself. In return he gave me his bottle, and I took two swallows.

How are things? I asked him.

I'm still waiting for my family to send me the money to go back to Istanbul. He filled the pipe and handed it to me. I passed the bottle back to him. We went on drinking, smoking, and discussing our troubles, until all the whisky was gone.

What are you doing tonight? I asked him.

Nothing.

He hid the bottle under his jacket, and we went back downstairs. Abdelmalek was standing as usual, lecturing on the afternoon news broadcast in Arabic from London, which had just finished. My magazine was still lying on the table. I sat down and asked Kemal to have something with me. He excused himself, saying that he had an appointment with Mahmoud the Egyptian at the Café Dar Debbagh.

He's going to lend me some money, he said.

Moh came up to us suddenly, remarking: I don't like drunks in this place. Kemal, not understanding Arabic, answered: *Es salaam, Monsieur Moh.*

I burst out laughing. Kemal signalled goodbye and went out. Abdelmalek glared at me angrily and sat down.

Go on, go on, Si Abdelmalek, urged Afiouna.

How do you expect me to go on with that kid laughing?

I'm not a kid, I told him. And you talk about Mohamed Neguib and Gamal Abd el Nasser as if you had a conference with them every day. Where do you get all that stuff about them?

Shut up! Illiterate! he roared, beside himself. You want to talk about politics, you, when you can't even write your name?

Mesari was trying to get Abdelmalek's attention. Don't listen to him, he told him. He's drunk.

It seemed to me that this was a good opportunity to get in a blow at Abdelmalek and his group of friends. They wouldn't smoke with me, I thought, and I began to cast about for the words that would most annoy him. I could think of nothing to say. My mind was heavy with *kif, majoun,* and whisky. I'll have to ask him to go outside with me and fight. It's the easiest way. It involves no thinking of any kind.

I'm illiterate and ignorant, I said. But you're a liar. I'd rather be what I am than a liar like you.

Ah, get back to your pimping, he told me.

If you have a sexy sister, send her around. I'll find her somebody, I said.

No arguments in this café, Moh cried angrily, looking at me.

Why do you say it just to me? I asked him. Because he's a great professor and I'm only a stupid lout?

Come on, that's enough, said Grida. Get together and cheat the devil.

But the devil is people, I told him.

Then I turned to Abdelmalek. Listen, Zailachi. Come outside and I'll show you who the illiterate pimp is.

He jumped up and ran towards me. The three of them, Grida, Mesari and Afiouna, blocked his way, but he shoved them aside. I got up, holding my glass in my hand, and dashed the coffee into his face. He put his hands over his eyes. Someone grabbed me from behind.

Outside, Zailachi! I cried. The man behind me let me go.

Be sensible, Grida told me. This is no way to behave to somebody like him.

Who does he think he is here? He's just a student who couldn't stay in school, and now he's come to Tangier to live like a tramp.

I saw Mesari and someone else going up to the roof with Abdelmalek. I walked back to my table, and Afiouna sat down with me. He filled the *sebsi*, lit it, and handed it to me, saying: Here. Take it and smoke. It'll make you feel calmer.

I'm not drunk, and I'm not *m'hashish*, I told him. This isn't the first time I've had alcohol or *majoun*.

Then Grida went upstairs.

Nobody said you were drunk or *kiffed*, Afiouna said.

They think I am.

We all drink and smoke *kif*, he said.

I smoked the pipe and coughed a little. Afiouna got up and brought his glass of tea from the table where they had been sitting. I took a sip from it, and stopped coughing.

I've won the argument, I thought to myself. The other men in the café were discussing the altercation, and I noticed that certain of them agreed with me. They must already have felt the same way I did about Abdelmalek.

Grida came down the stairs, followed a moment later by Abdelmalek, Mesari, and his friend. Abdelmalek had washed the coffee from his face and clothes. Grida came over to me. You've got to make peace between you, he told me.

Yes, said Afiouna. Get up and talk to him. We're all friends here.

They insisted, and I rose. Mesari and his friend pushed Abdelmalek towards us, and we embraced. I turned to go back to my table, but they made me sit down with them.

Come on, Si Moh, give us something to drink, said Grida.

Kemal came staggering back into the café. He had a black eye.

Kemal! I said. What happened to you?

Moh stared at him with annoyance.

I got up and went over to him.

There were two of them, he said. They jumped on me. At a whorehouse in Bencharqi.

Why?

They took me for a Christian. They wouldn't believe I was a Moslem. They said how could I be a Moslem if I didn't speak Arabic?

But why?

I wanted to take a Moroccan girl in to bed.

All that trouble for a common whore, I said. Come and sit down with us.

No. You come with me.

Where?

We'll go to the Zoco Chico and have something to drink. Mahmoud lent me a little money.

I excused myself to Abdelmalek and his group, and went out with Kemal.

We went to the brothel run by Seoudiya el Kahala.

I know the woman who runs the place, I explained. And all the girls.

Hadija Srifiya let us in. She took us into a room and we sat down. Soon Seoudiya el Kahala came in and greeted me. I introduced her to Kemal.

*Es salaam*, he said.

Is he a Moslem? she asked me.

Naturally he is.

Does he speak Arabic?

No. He only knows a few words.

But how can he be a Moslem if he doesn't speak Arabic?

I told her there were other countries where the people were Moslems but spoke other languages.

*Ana Muslim*, Kemal told the two women. *Allah oua Mohamed rasoul illah.*

We all laughed. Sit down, Lalla Seoudiya told us. Do you want Hadija to stay here with you?

I asked Kemal. Of course she should stay, he said. Tell her to bring another pretty one.

We ordered a bottle of cognac and a bottle of soda water. I told Hadija to find us a girl who liked to drink and talk. The two women went out.

Do you like that one? I asked Kemal.

She's perfect. Moroccan girls look a lot like Turkish girls, you know.

Hadija came back carrying a tray with the drinks. Sfiya el Qasriya was with her.

She greeted me. How are you, handsome?

I introduced Kemal, and she sat down beside him.

The drinks are a hundred and twenty-five pesetas, said Hadija.

And if we add you two to the bill, how much will it be? I asked her.

She looked at Sfiya and giggled: Three hundred pesetas.

How much? Kemal asked me.

Three hundred altogether, for them and the drinks.

He pulled out two one-hundred peseta notes. This is all I've got, he said.

I took the two bills and added another. Call Lalla Seoudiya, I told Hadija.

Give me the money, she said. Don't you trust me?

It's not that. I just want to get everything straight with Lalla Seoudiya.

Ah! I see. Well, do as you like.

Sit down, I said. I'm going to fix it up with her.

I went out of the room in search of Lalla Seoudiya. She

was sitting in a far corner of the patio. I want to pay you now for the drinks and the girls, I told her.

You know how much it is, she said. Two hundred and fifty pesetas. That's the price I make especially for you, because you're an old client.

I gave her the money, and asked her to have me called at half past six in the morning. I explained that the four of us would be using the same room.

When I got back to Kemal, he had Sfiya's head between his hands, and was stroking her cheeks and kissing her tenderly. It's as if he was afraid she was going to get away, I said to myself. Perhaps some day I'll sleep with a Turkish girl.

Hadija wanted to know if I had got everything arranged with Lalla Seoudiya. I folded a fifty-peseta note very small and slipped it into her hand, saying: Keep it. It's for you. Everything's all settled. She stuffed the money into her bodice and kissed me on the cheek.

I was just dropping off to sleep when Hadija, lying beside me, said: Did you hear that? Sfiya says your friend the Turk is licking her with his tongue.

Let him do what he likes with her, I said.

I'd rather have a tongue lick me than a *zib* massage me, Sfiya called out. The two girls laughed.

I want to go to sleep, I told Hadija. I've got to get up early and go down to the port.

Don't worry, she said. I'll wake you up as early as you like. I'm a light sleeper. She turned towards me and hugged me. Then she pushed my bent knee between her legs and began to rub herself against it. She wishes it were a *zib*, I thought.

Sfiya had started to moan, and Hadija increased her efforts against my knee. Suddenly she pulled at my hair violently. Then she relaxed. Kemal and Sfiya were laughing together.

Hadija turned over and lay face down. I put out my hand and ran it lightly over her buttocks. She was still pushing herself slowly back and forth against the mattress. I became excited again, and jumped onto her back for a ride. She tried to throw me from my seat, but I held tight and stayed astride. I pretended to myself that if I were unseated I should fall into emptiness. I was on a flying she-camel high over the desert, and to fall off would mean being lost in the wilderness.

In the morning when I returned from the port I went into a bookshop in Oued el Ahardan and bought a book that explained the essentials of writing and reading Arabic.

I found Abdelmalek at the Café Moh with his brother Hassan from Larache. I apologized again for what had happened the night before. Forget it, he said. I was in a bad mood too.

They asked me to sit down with them, and I showed Abdelmalek the book I had bought. I've got to learn to read and write, I said. Your brother Hamid showed me a few letters while we were in the Comisaría together. He said I could learn easily.

Why not?

Would you like to go to school in Larache? asked Hassan.

School? Me? I said surprised. It's impossible. I'm twenty years old and I can't read a word.

That doesn't matter. I know the head of a school down there. I'll give you a note to him. He'll take you. He has a soft spot for out-of-towners who want to study. If I didn't have to go to Tetuan with this trouble I could take you myself to see him.

He paused, and then said: Why don't you go and buy an envelope and a sheet of paper, and I'll write you the note.

I did not believe in any of this, but I did as he suggested, and hurried back to the café. He laid the sheet of paper on top of a periodical, and began to write. From time to time he stopped and smoked a pipe of *kif* with us. When he had finished he folded the paper and put it into the envelope. Then he handed it to me.

When should I go to Larache to see him? I asked Hassan.

Whenever you like. But try and go soon.

It was about noon when Hassan said goodbye to us, and went out to catch the bus to Tetuan. As he shook my hand he said: Be sure and go to Larache. I'll look for you down there in a few days.

When he had gone, Abdelmalek said: I've got to go up to the graveyard at Bou Araqia.

What for? I asked him.

I promised some of my friends here in the café I'd chant some *surat* today. One of them is Afiouna. His mother's buried there.

I'll go with you, I said. Would you be able to chant a *surah* at my brother's grave?

Your brother?

I have a brother buried there.

We smoked two pipes and then went out. On the way I asked him: What happened with Hassan? What trouble has he got in Tetuan?

He's crazy. They found him drinking wine and smoking *kif* in the students' dormitory at the mosque.

Tough luck!

He's always doing stupid things like that.

As we went through the Zoco de Fuera I bought a bunch of flowers, and at the gateway to the cemetery a sprig of myrtle. Inside we found a few *tolba* chanting. The relatives of the dead stood listening. We wandered among the graves.

Do you know where each grave is? Each one you're going to chant for?

No, he said. It's the idea that's important. I don't have to be standing beside a grave to chant to it. Where's your brother's grave?

I looked towards the wall at whose base Abdelqader had been buried.

It's impossible to find it, I told him. We never made him a gravestone before we went to Tetuan. There was no money. My father had just got out of jail, and my mother was selling vegetables in the Zoco de Fuera.

We climbed to the top of a small hill, and Abdelmalek began to chant the verses for the relatives of his friends. When he had finished, he asked me: Which part was he buried in?

Then we walked down towards the ruined wall. Over this way, near this wall, I said.

He intoned: *Ya sin oual Qoran el Hakim* . . . while I laid the flowers on several nearby graves. My brother is buried somewhere here, I said to myself. Maybe under my feet, or under Abdelmalek's feet. And the words Abdelmalek is chanting, what are they for? My little brother never had a chance to sin. All he did was to live his illness. The old man who had helped to bury him had told me: Your brother is with the angels. Has he become an angel, perhaps? And I, what shall I become? A devil, most likely. They say the little ones are angels and the big ones are devils, and it's too late for me to be an angel.